School Subject-Integrated Reading Series

Reading for Subject

SECOND EDITION

1

Reading for Subject 1

Publisher Chung Kyudo
Authors Ko Miseon, Kim Haeja, Michael A. Putlack
Editors Seo Jeong-ah, Jeong Yeonsoon
Designers Koo Soojung, Forest

First published in December 2021
By Darakwon, Inc.
Darakwon Bldg., 211, Munbal-ro, Paju-si, Gyeonggi-do 10881
Republic of Korea
Tel: 82-2-736-2031 (Ext. 250)
Fax: 82-2-732-2037

ISBN 978-89-277-0896-4 54740
978-89-277-0895-7 54740 (set)

www.darakwon.co.kr

Photo Credits
Nicku (p.19), Jaroslav Moravcik (p.35), Anagoria (p.43), Viacheslav Lopatin (p.51), Anton_Ivanov (p.54), Hayk_Shalunts (p.55), Pavel L Photo and Video (p.59), Ronrosano (p.63), Fæ (p.95), kiraziku2u (p.98), Sikander (p.99), Big Joe (p.102), travelview (p.107) / www.shutterstock.com

Components Main Book / Workbook
9 8 7 6 5 4 3 23 24 25 26 27

School Subject-Integrated Reading Series

Reading for Subject

SECOND EDITION

1

How to Use This Book

This book has 5 chapters, and each consists of 4 units. At the end of a chapter, there is a writing activity with a topic related to the last unit.

Student Book

Two warm-up questions to encourage students to think about the topic of the unit

QR code for listening to the reading passage

Finding the topic of each paragraph

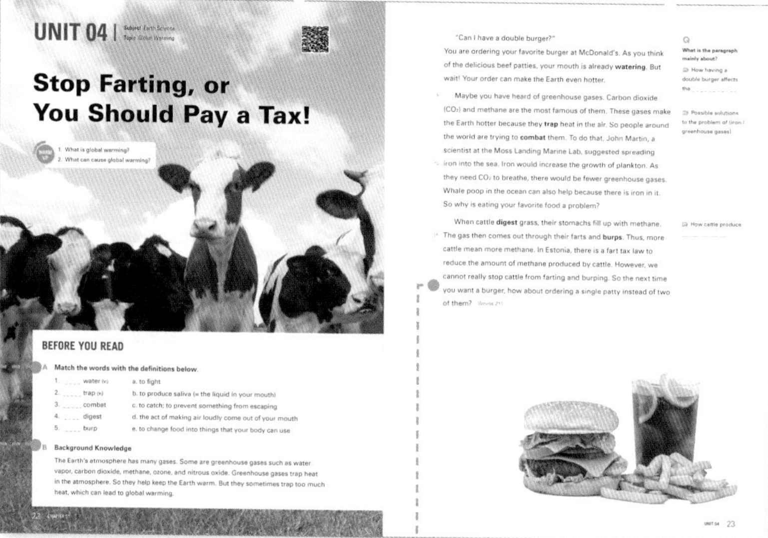

BEFORE YOU READ

Students can learn the meaning of key vocabulary words by matching the words with their definitions.

Background knowledge about the topic is provided to help students better understand the main reading passage.

MAIN READING PASSAGE

Interesting, informative nonfiction reading passages covering various school subjects are provided.

CHECK YOUR COMPREHENSION

This section asks students to identify the main ideas and details and to make accurate inferences from the passage through 4 multiple-choice and 2 short-answer questions.

CHECK YOUR COMPREHENSION

SHOW YOUR COMPREHENSION

SUMMARIZE YOUR READING

SHOW YOUR COMPREHENSION

Students can remember what they have read and organize the key information in the passage in a visual manner.

SUMMARIZE YOUR READING

Students can review and practice summarizing the key information in the passage.

THINK & WRITE

Students can strengthen their writing skills by connecting ideas from the passage to their own lives. This also helps students prepare themselves for English performance assessments in school.

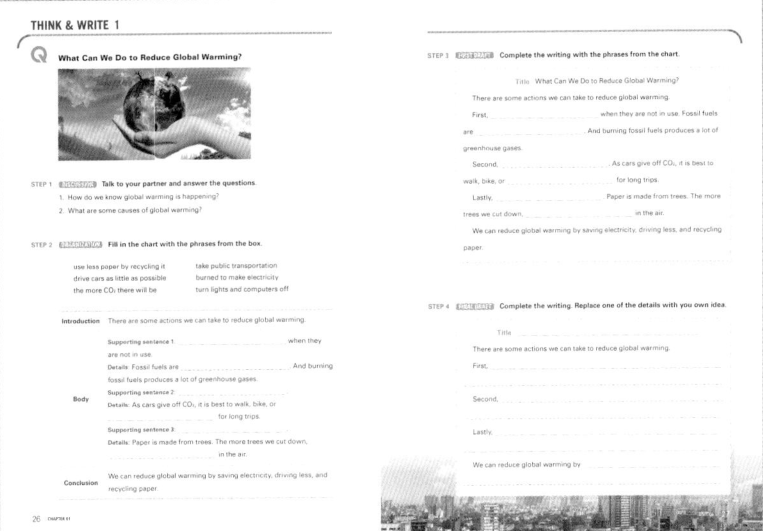
THINK & WRITE 1

What Can We Do to Reduce Global Warming?

STEP 1 **Talk to your partner and answer the questions.**

1. How do we know global warming is happening?
2. What are some causes of global warming?

STEP 2 **Fill in the chart with the phrases from the box.**

use less paper by recycling it / take public transportation / drive cars as little as possible / burned to make electricity / the more CO_2 there will be / turn lights and computers off

Introduction	There are some actions we can take to reduce global warming.
Body	**Supporting sentence 1**: ____ when they are not in use. **Details**: Fossil fuels are ____. And burning fossil fuels produces a lot of greenhouse gases. **Supporting sentence 2**: ____ **Details**: As cars give off CO_2, it is best to walk, bike, or ____ for long trips. **Supporting sentence 3**: ____ **Details**: Paper is made from trees. The more trees we cut down, ____ in the air.
Conclusion	We can reduce global warming by saving electricity, driving less, and recycling paper.

26 CHAPTER 01

STEP 3 **Complete the writing with the phrases from the chart.**

Title What Can We Do to Reduce Global Warming?

There are some actions we can take to reduce global warming.

First, ____ when they are not in use. Fossil fuels are ____. And burning fossil fuels produces a lot of greenhouse gases.

Second, ____. As cars give off CO_2, it is best to walk, bike, or ____ for long trips.

Lastly, ____. Paper is made from trees. The more trees we cut down, ____ in the air.

We can reduce global warming by saving electricity, driving less, and recycling paper.

STEP 4 **Complete the writing. Replace one of the details with you own idea.**

Title ____

There are some actions we can take to reduce global warming.

First, ____

Second, ____

Lastly, ____

We can reduce global warming by ____

Workbook

Students can review the vocabulary they learn in each unit. They can also review key structures in the passages by translating sentences and by putting words in the correct order.

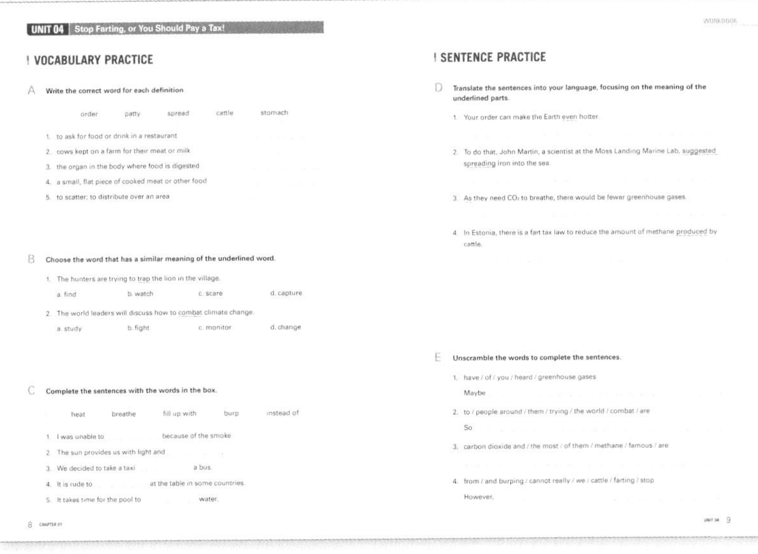
UNIT 04 Stop Farting, or You Should Pay a Tax!

VOCABULARY PRACTICE

A **Write the correct word for each definition**

order / patty / spread / cattle / stomach

1. to ask for food or drink in a restaurant
2. cows kept on a farm for their meat or milk
3. the organ in the body where food is digested
4. a small, flat piece of cooked meat or other food
5. to scatter; to distribute over an area

B **Choose the word that has a similar meaning of the underlined word.**

1. The hunters are trying to trap the lion in the village.
   a. find b. watch c. scare d. capture
2. The world leaders will discuss how to combat climate change.
   a. study b. fight c. monitor d. change

C **Complete the sentences with the words in the box.**

heat / breathe / fill up with / burp / instead of

1. I was unable to ____ because of the smoke.
2. The sun provides us with light and ____.
3. We decided to take a taxi ____ a bus.
4. It is rude to ____ at the table in some countries.
5. It takes time for the pool to ____ water.

8 CHAPTER 01

WORKBOOK

SENTENCE PRACTICE

D **Translate the sentences into your language, focusing on the meaning of the underlined parts.**

1. Your order can make the Earth even hotter.
2. To do that, John Martin, a scientist at the Moss Landing Marine Lab, suggested spreading iron into the sea.
3. As they need CO_2 to breathe, there would be fewer greenhouse gases.
4. In Estonia, there is a fart tax law to reduce the amount of methane produced by cattle.

E **Unscramble the words to complete the sentences.**

1. have / of / you / heard / greenhouse gases
   Maybe ____
2. to / people around / them / trying / the world / combat / are
   So ____
3. carbon dioxide and / the most / of them / methane / famous / are
4. from / and burping / cannot really / we / cattle / farting / stop
   However, ____

UNIT 04 9

Table of Contents

CHAPTER
01

UNIT 01 The Rainbow Tree _ Life Science

UNIT 02 A Tragedy of Love _ History

UNIT 03 Be Smarter Through Mozart's Music _ Art & Music

UNIT 04 Stop Farting, or You Should Pay a Tax! _ Earth Science

THINK & WRITE 1

What Can We Do to Reduce Global Warming?

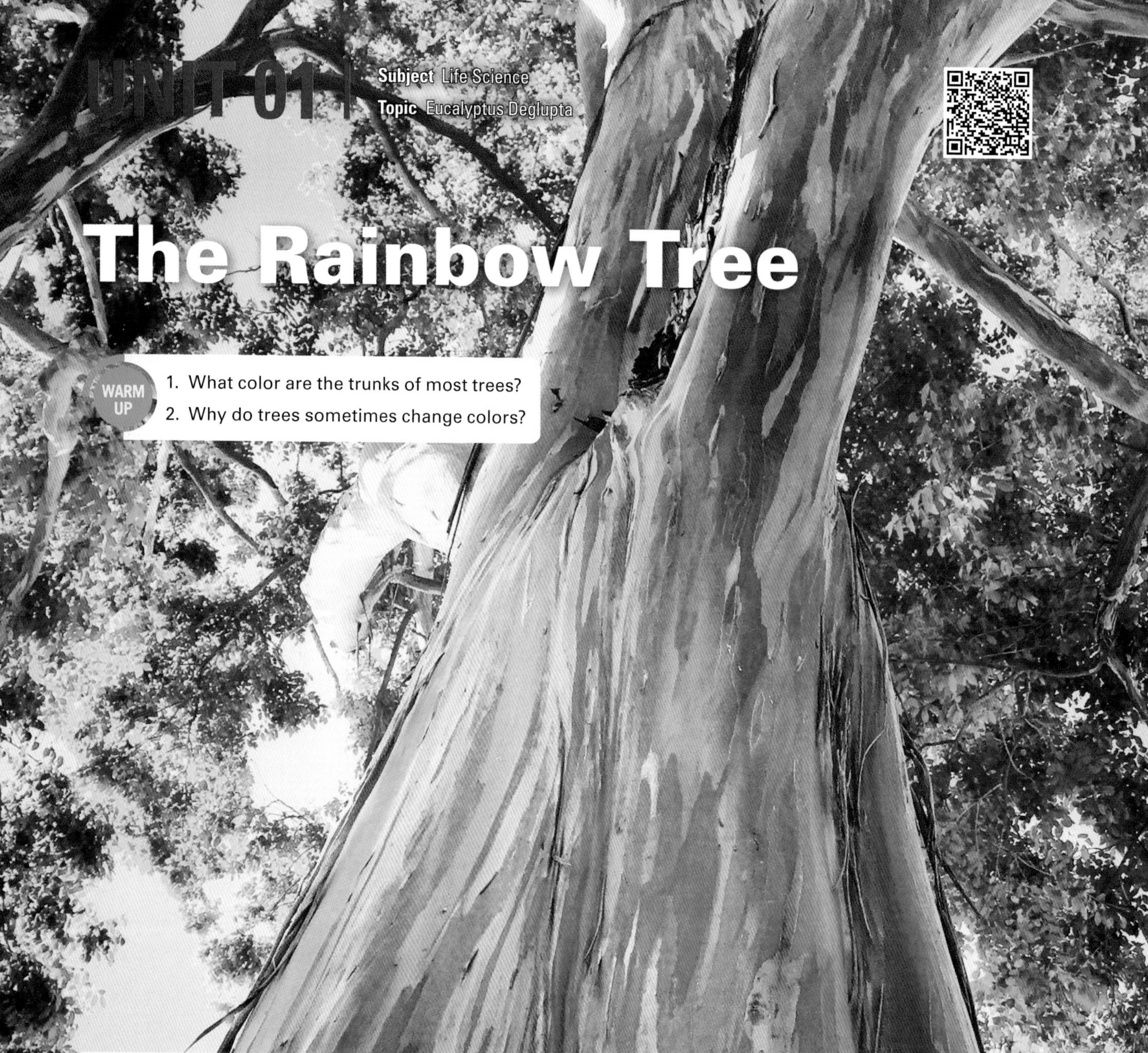

The Rainbow Tree

WARM UP

1. What color are the trunks of most trees?
2. Why do trees sometimes change colors?

BEFORE YOU READ

A Match the words with the definitions below.

1. ______ species
2. ______ shed
3. ______ trunk
4. ______ pigment
5. ______ visible

a. able to be seen
b. a type or kind of plant or animal
c. to lose something naturally
d. the thick stem of a tree
e. a substance that gives color to other materials

B Background Knowledge

Eucalyptus trees are tropical plants that mainly grow in Australia. Most people know them because koalas eat their leaves. However, they have other uses. People use eucalyptus oil as a medicine and cleaner as well as for other uses. Their leaves can also help people with breathing problems.

The eucalyptus tree is native to Australia. There are many **species** of the tree though. One species, the rainbow eucalyptus, is considered the most beautiful tree in the world. It grows in Hawaii, the Philippines, Indonesia, and Papua New Guinea.

The rainbow eucalyptus is a tall tree that **sheds** its bark every year. When the bark falls off, people can see a layer of green on the **trunk**. After that, something amazing happens. A wide variety of colors appear. These include blue, purple, orange, red, and brown.

The bark does not all fall off at once. Instead, it falls off in pieces. The pieces form different colors, creating the tree's rainbow-like appearance. As a result, no two rainbow eucalyptus trees look the same.

Nobody is sure why this happens. One theory is that there is a thin layer of cells beneath the bark. People can see through that layer, so they can see the green chlorophyll in the trunk. The cells in the layer have a **pigment** called tannin. As the chlorophyll starts to disappear, the colors of the tannin become **visible**. As a result, the tree becomes a living work of art.

In some forests, the trees create a bright display of colors. It is a sight people will always remember. Words 212

Q

What is the paragraph mainly about?

P1 What the ______________ is and where it grows

P2 What happens when the (bark / leaves) of the tree falls off

P3 Why rainbow eucalyptus trees look (different / the same)

P4 One theory on why the tree changes ______________

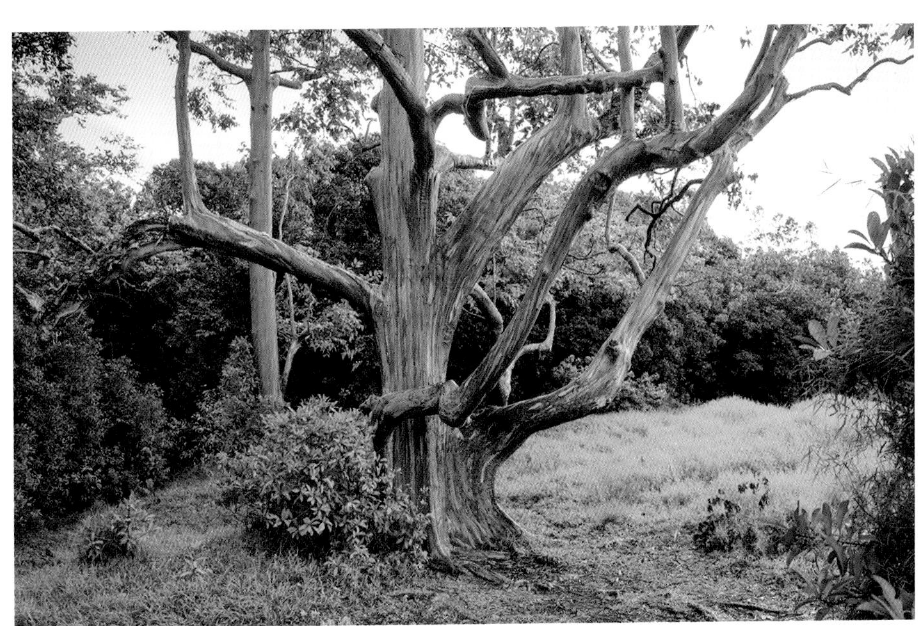

CHECK YOUR COMPREHENSION

Choose the best answers.

Main Idea

1 **What is the passage mainly about?**

a. The most popular kinds of eucalyptus trees
b. The reason the rainbow eucalyptus is so colorful
c. The different colors the rainbow eucalyptus can be
d. The effects of chlorophyll on the rainbow eucalyptus

Details

2 **The rainbow eucalyptus gets its name because of its ______________.**

a. roots
b. bark
c. leaves
d. flowers

3 **According to one theory, there is a layer of cells under the bark that have ______________.**

a. scent
b. tannin
c. poison
d. chlorophyll

4 **What can be inferred from the passage?**

a. Koalas eat the leaves of the rainbow eucalyptus.
b. The rainbow eucalyptus can be found in Australia.
c. The rainbow eucalyptus is the tallest tree in the world.
d. The color of the rainbow eucalyptus changes every year.

Write the answers in complete sentences.

5 **What can people see first when the bark of the rainbow eucalyptus falls off?**

____

6 **When do the colors of the tannin become visible?**

____

SHOW YOUR COMPREHENSION

Fill in the chart with the phrases from the box.

The Rainbow Eucalyptus

What It Is	• It is a tall tree that ❶ ______________. • It grows in Hawaii, the Philippines, Indonesia, and Papua New Guinea.
Why It Is Colorful	• There is ❷ ______________ beneath the bark. • The cells in the layer ❸ ______________. • As ❹ ______________, the colors of the tannin become visible.

a thin layer of cells
sheds its bark every year
the chlorophyll disappears
have a pigment called tannin

SUMMARIZE YOUR READING

Complete the summary with the words from the box.

in pieces   chlorophyll   remember   different
colors   tannin   beautiful   bark

The rainbow eucalyptus is a tall tree that grows in parts of Asia and the US. It is considered the most ❶ ______________ tree in the world. Its ❷ ______________ falls off every year. At first, people can see green. Then, it changes ❸ ______________ to blue, purple, orange, or other colors. The bark falls off ❹ ______________, so rainbow eucalyptus trees all look ❺ ______________. Nobody knows exactly why the tree changes colors. The reason might be that the ❻ ______________ in the tree disappears. Then, the pigment ❼ ______________ in the tree becomes visible. This creates a sight people will always ❽ ______________.

UNIT 02 | **Subject** History **Topic** The Taj Mahal

A Tragedy of Love

WARM UP

1. What does the Taj Mahal look like?
2. Why do you think the Taj Mahal was built?

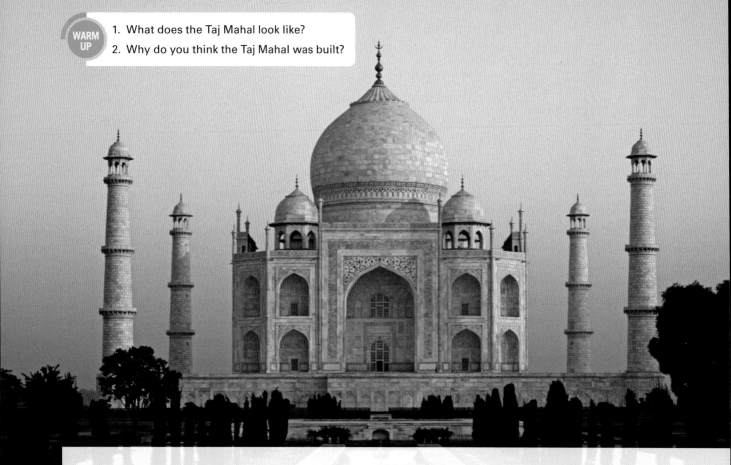

BEFORE YOU READ

A Match the words with the definitions below.

1. _____ emperor
2. _____ give birth to
3. _____ tomb
4. _____ poverty
5. _____ overthrow

a. the state of being poor
b. a man who rules a group of countries
c. to produce a baby or young animal
d. to remove a leader or king from power
e. a place where a dead person is buried

B Background Knowledge

The Taj Mahal is located in Agra, India. It looks like an Islamic mosque, a building where Muslims go to worship, but is a tomb. It was built for one of the wives of a Mughal emperor in the 1600s. The Taj Mahal is known for its beauty and is a UNESCO World Heritage Site.

A long time ago, Mughal **emperor** Shah Jahan in India got married to his third wife, Mumtaz Mahal. He loved her more than anyone else. In 1631, however, Mumtaz Mahal died while **giving birth to** their child. Before she died, she asked him to bury her in the most beautiful **tomb** in the world.

To keep his promise, Shah Jahan began to build the most beautiful tomb: the Taj Mahal. The construction began in 1631 and was completed around 1653. During the construction, twenty thousand workers and thousands of artisans and craftsmen were employed.

Soon after the completion, however, Shah Jahan cut off the artisans' and craftsmen's fingers. He was afraid that they would build the same tomb in another place. In addition, he spent so much money that people suffered from **poverty**. In 1657, Shah Jahan fell ill, and the next year, his son Aurangzeb **overthrew** him. After that, Shah Jahan was kept in Fort Agra, which overlooked the Taj Mahal.

Although Shah Jahan kept his promise to his wife, he cried all day while looking at her tomb. After his death, his son buried him next to his wife. Finally, Shah Jahan was in peace next to his wife.

Words 201

What is the paragraph mainly about?

P1 What Mumtaz Mahal asked ______________ to do

P2 The (construction / beauty) of the Taj Mahal

P3 What happened after the ______________ of the Taj Mahal

P4 (When / Where) Shah Jahan was buried

CHECK YOUR COMPREHENSION

Choose the best answers.

Main Idea

1 **What is the passage mainly about?**

a. Shah Jahan's cruelty
b. Why the Taj Mahal is famous
c. Aurangzeb's revenge on his father
d. The hidden truths of the Taj Mahal

Details

2 **According to the passage, which is NOT true about the Taj Mahal?**

a. It is located in India.
b. It took over 20 years to build.
c. Shah Jahan was buried there after he died.
d. Mumtaz Mahal saw the Taj Mahal before she died.

3 **The Taj Mahal was built as a tomb for ______________.**

a. Shah Jahan
b. Shah Jahan's son
c. Shah Jahan's wife
d. artisans and craftsmen

4 **What can be inferred from the passage?**

a. Shah Jahan had only one wife.
b. Shah Jahan was killed by his son.
c. The Taj Mahal was designed by Mumtaz Mahal.
d. Shah Jahan loved Mumtaz Mahal until he died.

Write the answers in complete sentences.

5 **What did Mumtaz Mahal ask Shah Jahan before she died?**

____

6 **Why did Shah Jahan cut off the artisans' and craftsmen's fingers?**

____

SHOW YOUR COMPREHENSION

Fill in the chart with the phrases from the box.

The Taj Mahal

How It Was Built	• ❶ ______________ asked him to bury her in the most beautiful tomb. • From 1631 to 1653, many ❷ ______________ were employed.
What Happened After the Completion	• The artisans' and craftsmen's fingers were cut off. • People ❸ ______________. • Shah Jahan was ❹ ______________.

suffered from poverty
overthrown by his son
Shah Jahan's third wife
workers, artisans, and craftsmen

SUMMARIZE YOUR READING

Complete the summary with the words from the box.

cut off | overthrew | employed | poverty
promise | miserable | in peace | third wife

The Taj Mahal is a tomb for Shah Jahan's ❶ ______________, Mumtaz Mahal. Although Shah Jahan kept his ❷ ______________ to build the most beautiful tomb for her, it made people ❸ ______________. From 1631 to 1653, a lot of workers, artisans, and craftsmen were ❹ ______________ to complete it. After the completion of the Taj Mahal, Shah Jahan ❺ ______________ the artisans' and craftsmen's fingers so that they would not build another tomb like it. People also suffered from ❻ ______________ because he spent all of the country's money. Then, Aurangzeb, his son, ❼ ______________ him while he was ill. Finally, he was ❽ ______________ after being buried next to his wife.

UNIT 03 | **Subject** Art & Music **Topic** The Mozart Effect

Be Smarter Through Mozart's Music

1. What kind of music do you like?
2. What do you think the Mozart Effect is?

BEFORE YOU READ

A Match the words with the definitions below.

1. ______ temporarily
2. ______ spatial
3. ______ mental
4. ______ depression
5. ______ disappear

a. a feeling of being unhappy
b. for a short time
c. relating to the mind
d. to be impossible to find
e. relating to the position, size, shape, etc. of something

B Background Knowledge

Wolfgang Amadeus Mozart was an Austrian composer who lived from 1756 to 1791. He began writing music at the age of five. During his short life, he composed more than 600 pieces of music. *The Marriage of Figaro*, *Don Giovanni*, and *The Magic Flute* are some of his greatest works.

If listening to a particular type of music made you smarter, would you like to listen to it? The Mozart Effect refers to the belief that listening to Mozart's music can make people smarter. It was once very popular with mothers. They played Mozart's music to their babies as much as possible.

▲Wolfgang Amadeus Mozart

Q
What is the paragraph mainly about?

P1 What the ______________ is

The Mozart Effect was first described by Alfred A. Tomatis in 1991. Then, in 1993, the researchers Shaw and Ky studied whether the Mozart Effect really worked. They found out that listening to Mozart's music **temporarily** increased people's **spatial** intelligence. However, the results were mistakenly stated that listening to Mozart's music increased people's IQs.

P2 How Mozart's music affects people's (emotions / intelligence)

In 1997, Don Campbell wrote in a book that Mozart's music might improve people's **mental** development. So Zell Miller, the governor of Georgia in the United States at that time, suggested giving a CD of Mozart's music to every child in Georgia. Don Campbell also said that stress and **depression** could be reduced and that people could be relaxed by listening to Mozart's music.

P3 Some (positive / negative) effects of Mozart's music

The popularity of the Mozart Effect has **disappeared** today. But it is certain that listening to Mozart's music helps you be calm and focus on your studies. Just try it! Words 200

P4 How listening to Mozart's music can ______________ people

CHECK YOUR COMPREHENSION

Choose the best answers.

Main Idea

1 **What is the passage mainly about?**

a. Theories on the Mozart Effect

b. Why people like Mozart's music

c. The benefits of listening to music

d. Why children should listen to classical music

Details

2 **Shaw and Ky found out that Mozart's music increases people's ________________.**

a. IQs

b. memories

c. musical talent

d. spatial intelligence

3 **According to the passage, which is true about the Mozart Effect?**

a. Don Campbell first explained the concept.

b. Zell Miller did not believe in the Mozart Effect.

c. The Mozart Effect is only partially true.

d. The Mozart Effect is still popular today.

4 **Which did Don Campbell NOT say that Mozart's music could do?**

a. Improve people's mental development

b. Improve people's health

c. Reduce stress and depression

d. Provide relaxation

Write the answers in complete sentences.

5 **What did mothers who believed in the Mozart Effect do?**

____

6 **What did Zell Miller suggest?**

____

SHOW YOUR COMPREHENSION

Fill in the chart with the phrases from the box.

The Mozart Effect

What It Is	• It refers to the belief that listening to Mozart's music can ❶ ______________.
Research and Theories	• Alfred A. Tomatis first ❷ ______________. • Shaw and Ky found out that Mozart's music temporarily increased ❸ ______________. • Don Campbell believed Mozart's music can help improve ❹ ______________ and reduce stress.

described the Mozart Effect
people's spatial intelligence
make people smarter
people's mental development

SUMMARIZE YOUR READING

Complete the summary with the words from the box.

positive temporarily stress misunderstood
described IQs smarter disappeared

The Mozart Effect was popular because people believed Mozart's music could make people ❶ ______________. Alfred A. Tomatis first ❷ ______________ this idea. Later, Shaw and Ky studied the Mozart Effect. They found out that listening to Mozart's music can ❸ ______________ increase people's spatial intelligence. However, people ❹ ______________ the results and believed Mozart's music increased people's ❺ ______________. In 1997, Don Campbell wrote that Mozart's music is good for people's mental development and for reducing ❻ ______________. Although the popularity of the Mozart Effect has ❼ ______________, it is still believed that listening to Mozart's music has some ❽ ______________ effects.

UNIT 04 | **Subject** Earth Science **Topic** Global Warming

Stop Farting, or You Should Pay a Tax!

WARM UP
1. What is global warming?
2. What can cause global warming?

BEFORE YOU READ

A Match the words with the definitions below.

1. ______ water (*v.*)
2. ______ trap (*v.*)
3. ______ combat
4. ______ digest
5. ______ burp

a. to fight
b. to produce saliva (= the liquid in your mouth)
c. to catch; to prevent something from escaping
d. the act of making air loudly come out of your mouth
e. to change food into things that your body can use

B Background Knowledge

The Earth's atmosphere has many gases. Some are greenhouse gases such as water vapor, carbon dioxide, methane, ozone, and nitrous oxide. Greenhouse gases trap heat in the atmosphere. So they help keep the Earth warm. But they sometimes trap too much heat, which can lead to global warming.

"Can I have a double burger?"

You are ordering your favorite burger at McDonald's. As you think of the delicious beef patties, your mouth is already **watering**. But wait! Your order can make the Earth even hotter.

Maybe you have heard of greenhouse gases. Carbon dioxide (CO_2) and methane are the most famous of them. These gases make the Earth hotter because they **trap** heat in the air. So people around the world are trying to **combat** them. To do that, John Martin, a scientist at the Moss Landing Marine Lab, suggested spreading iron into the sea. Iron would increase the growth of plankton. As they need CO_2 to breathe, there would be fewer greenhouse gases. Whale poop in the ocean can also help because there is iron in it. So why is eating your favorite food a problem?

When cattle **digest** grass, their stomachs fill up with methane. The gas then comes out through their farts and **burps**. Thus, more cattle mean more methane. In Estonia, there is a fart tax law to reduce the amount of methane produced by cattle. However, we cannot really stop cattle from farting and burping. So the next time you want a burger, how about ordering a single patty instead of two of them? Words 211

Q

What is the paragraph mainly about?

P1 How having a double burger affects the ______________

P2 Possible solutions to the problem of (iron / greenhouse gases)

P3 How cattle produce ______________

CHECK YOUR COMPREHENSION

Choose the best answers.

Main Idea

1 **What is the passage mainly about?**

a. Types of greenhouse gases

b. Why the Earth is getting hotter

c. Some efforts to reduce greenhouse gases

d. How to increase the amount of plankton in the sea

Details

2 **According to the passage, which is true?**

a. Iron makes more greenhouse gases.

b. Plankton increase the amount of CO_2.

c. In Estonia, people have to pay taxes on their cows.

d. Whales are the animals most responsible for global warming.

3 **Eating less beef can help reduce ______________________.**

a. iron in the sea

b. global warming

c. the taxes people pay

d. the amount of plankton

4 **Which is NOT a thing that makes the Earth hotter?**

a. CO_2

b. Cattle

c. Methane

d. Whale poop

Write the answers in complete sentences.

5 **What did John Martin suggest to reduce greenhouse gases?**

____

6 **Why does Estonia have a fart tax law?**

____

SHOW YOUR COMPREHENSION

Fill in the chart with the phrases from the box.

How to Help Reduce Greenhouse Gases

Reduce CO_2	• by increasing the amount of ❶ ______ - ❷ ______ - whale poop in the ocean
Reduce Methane	• by reducing the amount of ❸ ______ - ❹ ______ - eating less beef

the fart tax law in Estonia
plankton in the sea
spreading iron into the sea
methane produced by cattle

SUMMARIZE YOUR READING

Complete the summary with the words from the box.

less beef　CO_2　combat　methane
iron　burps　heat　fart tax law

Greenhouse gases trap ❶ ______ in the air and make the Earth hotter. CO_2 and ❷ ______ are two of these gases. People are trying to ❸ ______ the gases to cool the Earth. As plankton need ❹ ______ to breathe, a scientist suggested spreading ❺ ______ into the sea to increase the amount of plankton. Eating ❻ ______ can also help reduce methane. The reason is that cattle give off a lot of methane through their farts and ❼ ______. In an effort to do this, Estonia has a(n) ❽ ______.

THINK & WRITE 1

What Can We Do to Reduce Global Warming?

STEP 1 **DISCUSSION** **Talk to your partner and answer the questions.**

1. How do we know global warming is happening?
2. What are some causes of global warming?

STEP 2 **ORGANIZATION** **Fill in the chart with the phrases from the box.**

use less paper by recycling it	take public transportation
drive cars as little as possible	burned to make electricity
the more CO_2 there will be	turn lights and computers off

Introduction	There are some actions we can take to reduce global warming.
Body	**Supporting sentence 1:** ______________ when they are not in use. **Details:** Fossil fuels are ______________. And burning fossil fuels produces a lot of greenhouse gases. **Supporting sentence 2:** ______________. **Details:** As cars give off CO_2, it is best to walk, bike, or ______________ for long trips. **Supporting sentence 3:** ______________. **Details:** Paper is made from trees. The more trees we cut down, ______________ in the air.
Conclusion	We can reduce global warming by saving electricity, driving less, and recycling paper.

STEP 3 FIRST DRAFT **Complete the writing with the phrases from the chart.**

Title What Can We Do to Reduce Global Warming?

There are some actions we can take to reduce global warming.

First, ______________________ when they are not in use. Fossil fuels are ______________________. And burning fossil fuels produces a lot of greenhouse gases.

Second, ______________________. As cars give off CO_2, it is best to walk, bike, or ______________________ for long trips.

Lastly, ______________________. Paper is made from trees. The more trees we cut down, ______________________ in the air.

We can reduce global warming by saving electricity, driving less, and recycling paper.

STEP 4 FINAL DRAFT **Complete the writing. Replace one of the details with you own idea.**

Title ______________________

There are some actions we can take to reduce global warming.

First, ______________________

____

Second, ______________________

____

Lastly, ______________________

____

We can reduce global warming by ______________________

____

CHAPTER 02

UNIT 05 | Subject Art & Music
Topic Colors

Colors, Colors, Colors

WARM UP
1. What is your favorite color?
2. What colors can you see around you?

BEFORE YOU READ

A Match the words with the definitions below.

1. ______ hue
2. ______ primary
3. ______ tertiary
4. ______ combine
5. ______ magenta

a. a reddish-purple color
b. a color; a tint
c. first; of the first order
d. third; of the third order
e. to put two or more things together

B Background Knowledge

Most people can see between twenty and thirty-two distinct colors. However, there are millions of tints and shades of colors. Tints are made by adding white to a color. Shades are made by adding black to a color. The human eye can see several million tints and shades of colors.

Look at the world around you. What colors can you see? The room you are inside may have colors such as red, blue, green, yellow, and brown. There are probably even more colors. Interestingly, these **hues** all originate from three colors.

Most colors are created by mixing two or more together. However, three colors cannot be created that way. They are the **primary** colors: red, yellow, and blue. While these three cannot be made from other colors, they are actually the source of all other colors.

Take some red and yellow paint and mix the two together. You get orange. If you mix yellow and blue, you get green. And if you mix blue and red, the result is purple. The three colors formed by mixing two primary colors are called secondary colors.

These are not the only colors though. There are many others. The others are **tertiary** colors. They can be created by mixing one primary color with one secondary color or by **combining** two secondary colors. For instance, blue and purple make violet while red and purple make **magenta**.

All colors are primary, secondary, or tertiary. Would you like to create your own colors? Then get some paint and start mixing. Words 204

Q

What is the paragraph mainly about?

P2 The (two / three) primary colors

P3 How to make the ______ colors

P4 What ______ colors are and how to make them

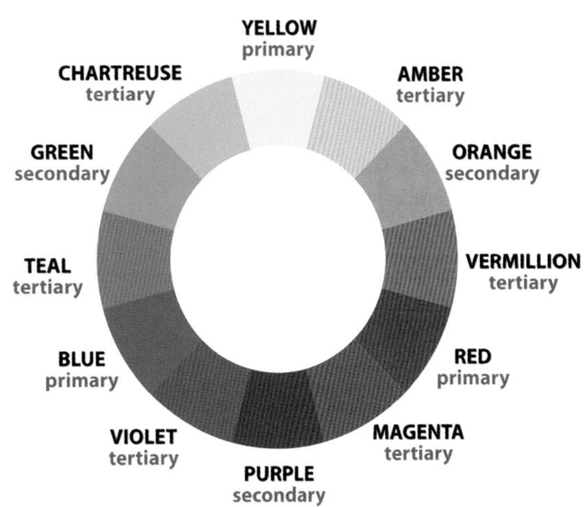

▲Color Wheel

CHECK YOUR COMPREHENSION

Choose the best answers.

Main Idea

1 **What is the passage mainly about?**

a. The different kinds of colors

b. The primary and secondary colors

c. The tertiary colors and making them

d. The importance of colors in our lives

Details

2 **According to the passage, which is NOT true about primary colors?**

a. There are only three of them.

b. They can be made from other colors.

c. They can combine to make secondary colors.

d. They include yellow and blue.

3 **You can make _______________ by combining blue and purple.**

a. red

b. violet

c. green

d. magenta

4 **What can be inferred from the passage?**

a. Red and yellow are the two most common colors.

b. Some people cannot see all of the different colors.

c. There are more tertiary colors than secondary colors.

d. White and black are both considered primary colors.

Write the answers in complete sentences.

5 **Where do all colors originate from?**

____

6 **How can tertiary colors be made?**

____

SHOW YOUR COMPREHENSION

Fill in the chart with the phrases from the box.

Colors	
Primary Colors	• are red, yellow, and blue • cannot be made from other colors • are ❶ ______________
Secondary Colors	• are ❷ ______________ • are made by mixing two primary colors
Tertiary Colors	• are made by mixing one primary color with one secondary color or by combining ❸ ______________ • include ❹ ______________

violet and magenta
orange, green, and purple
two secondary colors
the sources of all other colors

SUMMARIZE YOUR READING

Complete the summary with the words from the box.

secondary colors   orange   primary colors   mixing
magenta   tertiary colors   blue   combinations

There are probably many colors in the room that you are in. However, all colors come from just three colors: red, yellow, and ❶ ______________. They are the ❷ ______________. We can combine the primary colors to make ❸ ______________. For example, red and yellow make ❹ ______________ while yellow and blue make green. ❺ ______________ blue and red makes purple. Orange, green, and purple are the three secondary colors. The other colors are ❻ ______________. They are ❼ ______________ of one primary color and one secondary color. Or we can make them by combining two secondary colors. Violet and ❽ ______________ are two examples of tertiary colors.

UNIT 06 | **Subject** Language **Topic** The Rosetta Stone

The Rosetta Stone

WARM UP
1. What is the Rosetta Stone?
2. Why is the Rosetta Stone so important?

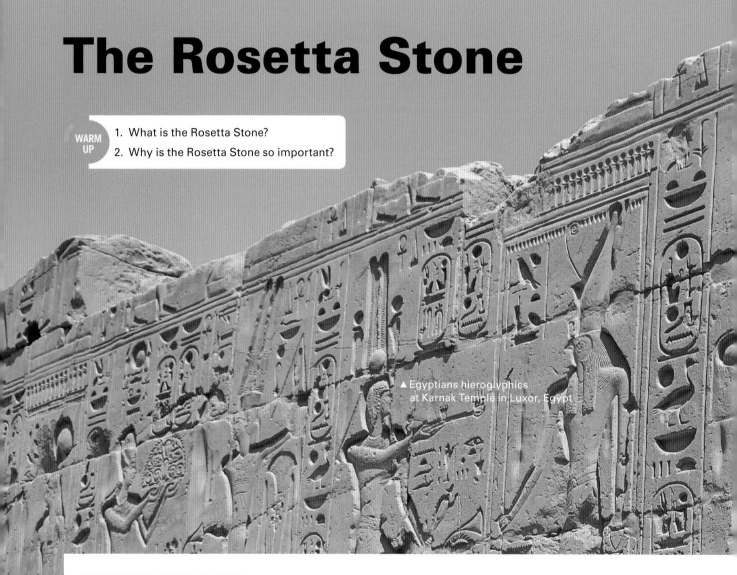

▲ Egyptians hieroglyphics at Karnak Temple in Luxor, Egypt

BEFORE YOU READ

A Match the words with the definitions below.

1. ______ compare
2. ______ script
3. ______ decipher
4. ______ stand for
5. ______ civilization

a. a particular writing system
b. to mean; to represent
c. to be able to read or understand
d. a society that is well organized and developed
e. to tell the similarities between two things

B Background Knowledge

The ancient Egyptians used a writing system called hieroglyphics. Each picture or symbol stood for a word or sound. There are more than 2,000 hieroglyphs. Few people in ancient Egypt could read hieroglyphics. Knowledge of how to read them was lost for centuries until the Rosetta Stone was deciphered.

You may not feel good if someone **compares** you to a stone. However, if it is the Rosetta Stone, you will be happy. This term often refers to a key to solving a problem.

In 1799, some soldiers in Napoleon's army dug up a strange black stone in Rosetta, Egypt. On the stone, there was the same message written in three different **scripts**: Egyptian *hieroglyphics, *demotic, and also Greek. Scholars in those days already knew the Greek language. So they thought that they could **decipher** the Egyptian languages soon. Many scholars worked on it and deciphered the demotic first. However, it was not easy to understand the hieroglyphics.

In 1822, the mystery finally began to be solved by French scholar Jean Francois Champollion. At that time, most scholars believed that hieroglyphics was picture writing. For example, they thought that a bird-shaped symbol always meant the word "bird." However, thinking differently, Champollion found out that a single picture symbol could **stand for** a sound as well as a word. For example, a bird-shaped symbol could also mean the sound "A."

Today, the Rosetta Stone is in the British Museum in London. Without it, we would not understand much about the ancient Egyptian language and **civilization**. Words 204

* **hieroglyphics** a system of writing that uses pictures instead of words, especially as used in ancient Egypt

* **demotic** the language used commonly in ancient Egypt

What is the paragraph mainly about?

P1 What the term ____________ means

P2 The (messages / languages) found on the Rosetta Stone

P3 What Jean Francois Champollion learned about ____________

P4 The (importance / appearance) of the Rosetta Stone

◀ The Rosetta Stone in the British Museum

CHECK YOUR COMPREHENSION

Choose the best answers.

Main Idea

1 **What is the passage mainly about?**

a. How the Rosetta Stone was found

b. The history of the Egyptian language

c. How the Egyptian language was deciphered

d. The importance of ancient Egyptian civilization

Details

2 **The writing on the Rosetta Stone was written in ______________ scripts.**

a. two

b. three

c. four

d. five

3 **According to the passage, which is NOT true about the Rosetta Stone?**

a. The stone was discovered in Egypt.

b. Napoleon wrote the writing on the stone.

c. Each message on the stone had the same meaning.

d. Today, the stone is not in Egypt.

4 **Why could most scholars NOT decipher the hieroglyphics on the Rosetta Stone?**

a. The stone was too damaged.

b. There were too many symbols.

c. They did not have enough time.

d. They thought it was picture writing.

Write the answers in complete sentences.

5 **What did Jean Francois Champollion find out about hieroglyphics?**

____

6 **Why is the Rosetta Stone important?**

____

SHOW YOUR COMPREHENSION

Write the numbers in the correct order.

The Rosetta Stone

a. Soldiers in Napoleon's army discovered a stone in Rosetta, Egypt. ______

b. They could decipher the demotic first. ______

c. He found out that the symbols could mean sounds as well as words. ______

d. Scholars tried hard to decipher the Egyptian scripts on the stone. ______

e. Today, the term "Rosetta Stone" means a key to solving a problem. ______

f. Much later, a French scholar finally deciphered the hieroglyphics. ______

g. As a result, we could solve many of the mysteries of ancient Egypt. ______

SUMMARIZE YOUR READING

Complete the summary with the words from the box.

decipher   differently   sounds   solving a problem
ancient languages   key   Egypt   unknown

The Rosetta Stone was found in ❶ ______ in 1799. It had writing in ❷ ______ on it. Egyptian hieroglyphics was one of them. Scholars made efforts to ❸ ______ the language, but it was not easy. Finally, in 1822, a French scholar solved the mystery by thinking ❹ ______. He found out that the symbols could mean certain ❺ ______ as well as words. In those days, a lot about the ancient Egyptian language and culture was ❻ ______. But the stone provided a(n) ❼ ______ to understanding them. That is why the term "Rosetta Stone" refers to a key to ❽ ______.

UNIT 07 | **Subject** Life Science **Topic** Mutualism

Like a Big Sister!

1. How do you and your brother or sister help each other?
2. What plants and animals help one another?

BEFORE YOU READ

A Match the words with the definitions below.

1. ______ pretend	a. very unpleasant
2. ______ swollen	b. to act as if something is true
3. ______ patrol	c. larger than normal
4. ______ disturb	d. to move around to check that there is no trouble
5. ______ repellent (*a.*)	e. to interrupt; to bother

B Background Knowledge

Sometimes a plant or animal has a relationship with another plant or animal. In some cases, both of them benefit. This is called mutualism. One example of mutualism is bees and flowers. Bees get nectar from flowers. And flowers get pollinated by bees, so they can make seeds.

Owen has an older sister named Cathy. Cathy takes good care of Owen. So he often **pretends** to be her bodyguard. Normally, she is nice to him. But she scolds Owen when he gets out of control. This is common behavior between brothers and sisters. A similar type of behavior happens with bullhorn acacia trees and the ants living within them.

The acacia has **swollen** thorns. They look like a bull's horns. The ants hollow them out, and the thorns become the ants' homes. The tree also produces delicious nectar that the ants eat. In return, the ants **patrol** on and around the tree to protect it. If other insects try to eat the leaves, the ants will attack the invaders.

Sometimes the tree has to control the ants though. The tree must be *pollinated in order to make seeds. Pollination usually happens thanks to insects such as bees. So the tree's flowers produce sweet nectar to attract bees. However, any ants near the flowers may **disturb** the bees. So the tree gives the ants more nectar on its stems. But what if the ants still move onto the flowers? Then the tree has to control them. It produces chemicals that are **repellent** to ants. Words 205

▲ A bee pollinating a flower

* **pollinate** to give a plant pollen so that it can make seeds

Q

What is the paragraph mainly about?

P1 How Cathy (scolds / takes care of) Owen

P2 How ____________ and the bullhorn acacia tree help one another

P3 How the bullhorn acacia tree ____________ ants

CHECK YOUR COMPREHENSION

Choose the best answers.

Main Idea

1 **What is the passage mainly about?**

a. The origin of the name bullhorn acacia

b. How the bullhorn acacia tree controls ants

c. How pollination occurs in the bullhorn acacia tree

d. The relationship between ants and the bullhorn acacia tree

Details

2 **According to the passage, which is NOT true?**

a. The acacia tree gets its name from its thorns.

b. Ants live within the acacia tree's thorns.

c. Ants help pollinate the acacia tree.

d. The acacia tree and ants benefit from one another.

3 **The acacia tree needs the help of bees to ______________.**

a. make seeds

b. make nectar

c. attack invaders

d. control the ants

4 **When does the acacia tree give ants more nectar?**

a. When the ants attack invaders

b. When the ants try to eat its leaves

c. When its flowers have produced too much nectar

d. When it has to keep the ants from going onto its flowers

Write the answers in complete sentences.

5 **What are the two things that the acacia tree gives ants?**

____

6 **What does the acacia tree do when it has to control ants?**

____

SHOW YOUR COMPREHENSION

Fill in the chart with the phrases from the box.

Ants and the Bullhorn Acacia Tree	
What Ants Do	• protect ❶ ________________ • disturb the bees ❷ ________________
What the Bullhorn Acacia Tree Does	• gives the ants ❸ ________________ • gives the ants more nectar on its stems during pollination • ❹ ________________ to control the ants

homes and nectar
produces chemicals
the tree from other insects
pollinating the flowers

SUMMARIZE YOUR READING

Complete the summary with the words from the box.

guard · takes care of · disturb · unpleasant · similar · nectar · scolds · safe

A big sister normally ❶ ________________ her younger brother, and her younger brother tries to keep her ❷ ________________. But when he gets out of control, she ❸ ________________ him. A(n) ❹ ________________ relationship occurs between the bullhorn acacia tree and the ants living within it. The tree provides the ants with homes and ❺ ________________. In return, the ants ❻ ________________ the tree. However, if the ants go onto the flowers and ❼ ________________ insects pollinating the flowers, the tree gives the ants more nectar on its stems. But if the ants still get out of control, the tree releases ❽ ________________ chemicals.

UNIT 08 |

Subject Social Students
Topic The Nuremberg Bridal Cup

A Symbol of Love in Germany

WARM UP
1. Why do people get married?
2. What are some wedding customs you know about?

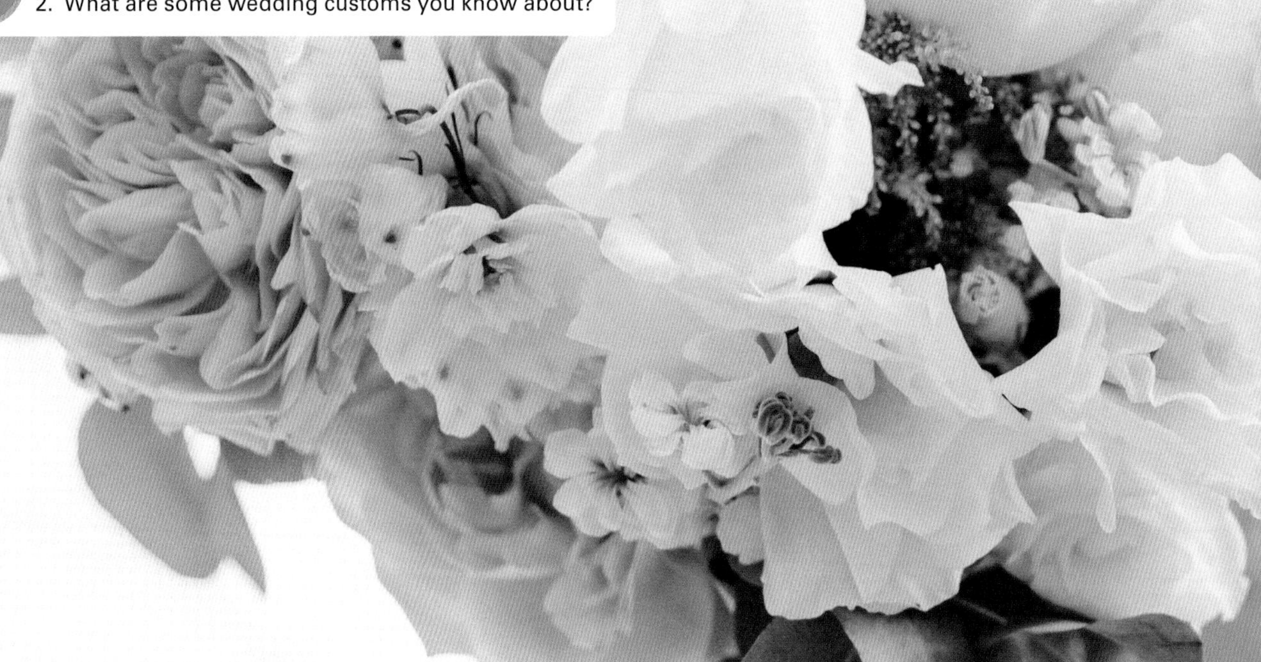

BEFORE YOU READ

A Match the words with the definitions below.

1. ______ noble — a. a suggestion
2. ______ goldsmith — b. a man who is getting married
3. ______ proposal — c. belonging to a high social class
4. ______ bride — d. a woman who is getting married
5. ______ groom — e. a person whose job is to make things with gold

B Background Knowledge

Around the world, every culture has its own unique customs for weddings. For example, some weddings are held in churches or temples while others take place in people's homes. The bride and the groom may wear unique clothes, too. These customs result in very different weddings around the world.

A long time ago in Nuremberg, Germany, a girl from a **noble** family fell in love with a young **goldsmith**. Her father became angry and put the goldsmith into an underground prison. However, that did not stop their love.

As the girl missed him, she became weak. So her father made a **proposal**. "Tell him to make a cup two people can drink from at the same time. Not a single drop should be spilled. Then, you can become his **bride**." People thought this task was impossible. But because of his true love, the goldsmith did it.

The cup was in the shape of a girl, and her skirt was hollowed out to serve as one cup. Her raised arms held a bucket, and it served as a second cup. As the second cup could *swivel, it could be filled at the same time and then face the second drinker. As a result, two people could drink without spilling anything, and the couple finally got married.

To this day, the cup, called the Nuremberg bridal cup, is a part of the German wedding tradition. At a wedding, if the bride and the **groom** drink without spilling anything, it is believed they will live happily ever after. Words 206

*swivel to turn around on a fixed position; to spin

Q

What is the paragraph mainly about?

P1 Why a girl's ____________ became angry with a goldsmith

P2 The kind of (cup / necklace) the goldsmith had to make

P3 (How / When) two people could drink from the cup together

P4 The tradition of the ____________ bridal cup

▲The Nuremberg bridal cup

CHECK YOUR COMPREHENSION

Choose the best answers.

Main Idea

1 **What is the passage mainly about?**

a. A skilled goldsmith in Germany

b. How to make a Nuremberg bridal cup

c. The origin of the Nuremberg bridal cup

d. Wedding traditions from around the world

Details

2 **According to the passage, which is NOT true about the girl's father?**

a. He put the goldsmith into a prison.

b. He tried to stop the couple from being together.

c. He proposed that the goldsmith make two cups.

d. He let the couple marry in the end.

3 **The cup in the passage is named after ________________________.**

a. the girl

b. the goldsmith

c. the girl's father

d. the place where it was made

4 **According to the passage, which is NOT true about the Nuremberg bridal cup?**

a. It is shaped like a girl with a bucket.

b. It consists of two cups.

c. Two people can drink from it together.

d. It is no longer used today.

Write the answers in complete sentences.

5 **Why did the girl's father make a proposal?**

____

6 **What does it mean if the bride and the groom drink from the cup without spilling anything at their wedding?**

____

SHOW YOUR COMPREHENSION

Write the numbers in the correct order.

The Nuremberg Bridal Cup

a. Surprisingly, the goldsmith could make such a cup. ________

b. A noble girl fell in love with a goldsmith. ________

c. He told the goldsmith to make a cup that two people could drink from at the same time. ________

d. Since then, the cup has become a part of the German wedding tradition. ________

e. One day, her father made a proposal. ________

f. However, her father tried to break them up. ________

g. Finally, the girl and the goldsmith got married. ________

SUMMARIZE YOUR READING

Complete the summary with the words from the box.

two people	wedding tradition	got married	impossible
goldsmith	live happily	spilling	true love

A long time ago, a noble girl loved a young ❶ ______________. Her father got angry and tried to break the couple up. He proposed that the young man make a cup that ❷ ______________ could drink from together. It seemed ❸ ______________ to make, but the goldsmith made one thanks to his ❹ ______________. Finally, the couple ❺ ______________. Since then, the cup has become a part of the German ❻ ______________. At a wedding, if a couple drinks from the cup without ❼ ______________ anything, people believe they will ❽ ______________ forever.

THINK & WRITE 2

What Are Some Things That Symbolize Love?

STEP 1 **DISCUSSION** **Talk to your partner and answer the questions.**

1. What gifts are often given as symbols of love?
2. What do you think a good way to express your love is?

STEP 2 **ORGANIZATION** **Fill in the chart with the phrases from the box.**

show his or her love	red roses also mean love
love each other forever	the most common symbol of love
wedding rings are symbols of love	heart shaped symbolizes love

Introduction	There are some things that symbolize love.
Body	**Supporting sentence 1:** ____________________. **Details:** The rings represent a promise that the bride and the groom will ____________________. **Supporting sentence 2:** ____________________. **Details:** When someone wants to ____________________, a bunch of red roses will help. **Supporting sentence 3:** Anything ____________________. **Details:** People believe that love starts from the heart. So it has been used as ____________________.
Conclusion	Wedding rings, red roses, and the heart mean love to people.

STEP 3 FIRST DRAFT **Complete the writing with the phrases from the chart.**

Title What Are Some Things That Symbolize Love?

There are some things that symbolize love.

First, ______________________________. The rings represent a promise that the bride and the groom will ______________________________.

Second, ______________________________. When someone wants to ______________________________, a bunch of red roses will help.

Lastly, anything ______________________________. People believe that love starts from the heart. So it has been used as ______________________________.

Wedding rings, red roses, and the heart mean love to people.

STEP 4 FINAL DRAFT **Complete the writing. Replace one of the details with you own idea.**

Title ______________________________

There are some things that symbolize love.

First, ______________________________

____

Second, ______________________________

____

Lastly, ______________________________

____

______________________________ mean love to people.

CHAPTER 03

UNIT 09 | Subject History Topic Pompeii

A Buried City

1. Are there any volcanoes in your country?
2. What is dangerous about volcanic eruptions?

▲ Mount Vesuvius

BEFORE YOU READ

A Match the words with the definitions below.

1. ______ destructive
2. ______ eruption
3. ______ excavation
4. ______ well preserved
5. ______ tourist attraction

a. the explosion of a volcano
b. causing great damage
c. being in good condition
d. a place that many tourists visit
e. the act of digging to find something from the past

B Background Knowledge

Natural disasters are events such as earthquakes, volcanic eruptions, floods, droughts, tornadoes, hurricanes, and tsunamis. They often cause a great amount of damage. They can destroy buildings and hurt and kill people. Sometimes areas affected by natural disasters take many years to recover.

Volcanoes, hurricanes, and earthquakes are called natural disasters because they cause people to die or to lose everything. It is true that nature is more powerful than humans. The following story shows how **destructive** natural disasters can be.

In 79 A.D., Pompeii, an ancient Roman city, was destroyed because of the **eruption** of Mount Vesuvius. Pliny the Younger, a writer and politician in ancient Rome, wrote a letter after he saw the eruption. In his letter, he described the tragic events of that day and the death of his uncle, Pliny the Elder, who tried to **rescue** people.

After the eruption, the city was buried under 4 to 6 meters of volcanic ash for about 1,500 years. It was rediscovered in 1599, and systematic **excavations** began in 1748. Because of the lack of air and moisture, the ruins of Pompeii had been **well preserved** for hundreds of years. So by looking at them, people can see how people in ancient Rome lived.

▲Victims of the eruption

Today, Pompeii is one of the most popular **tourist attractions** in Italy. About 2.5 million people visit the city every year. It also has UNESCO World Heritage Site status. Words 191

Q

What is the paragraph mainly about?

P1 Some examples of __________

P2 What (Pliny the Younger / Pliny the Elder) wrote about in a letter

P3 What happened to Pompeii after the __________

P4 What (Pompeii / Italy) is like today

CHECK YOUR COMPREHENSION

Choose the best answers.

Main Idea

1 **What is the passage mainly about?**

a. A letter by Pliny the Younger

b. Pompeii as a tourist attraction

c. How to prevent natural disasters

d. A city destroyed by a natural disaster

Details

2 **According to the passage, which is NOT true about Pompeii?**

a. It was destroyed by a volcano.

b. It stayed buried for about 1,500 years.

c. It was not discovered until 1748.

d. Its ruins were in good condition.

3 **The letter written by Pliny the Younger showed ____________________.**

a. how people in Pompeii lived

b. why Mount Vesuvius erupted

c. how terrible the volcanic eruption was

d. how Pompeii was before the volcanic eruption

4 **Why are the ruins of Pompeii important?**

a. They have great artistic value.

b. They contain expensive jewels.

c. They are the oldest ruins in the world.

d. They show how life in ancient Rome was.

Write the answers in complete sentences.

5 **What made the ruins of Pompeii well preserved for a long time?**

____

6 **What is Pompeii like today?**

____

SHOW YOUR COMPREHENSION

Fill in the chart with the phrases from the box.

The City of Pompeii

79 A.D.	• was destroyed by ❶ ______________ • was buried under volcanic ash for about 1,500 years
Rediscovery	• was rediscovered in 1599, and excavations began in 1748 • ❷ ______________ because of the lack of air and moisture • showed ❸ ______________
Present	• has become ❹ ______________ • has UNESCO World Heritage Site status

a tourist attraction in Italy
the eruption of Mount Vesuvius
had been well preserved
how people in ancient Rome lived

SUMMARIZE YOUR READING

Complete the summary with the words from the box.

volcanic ash　natural disasters　rediscovered　moisture
erupted　excavated　attractive　ancient Rome

There are many destructive ❶ ______________, and some are caused by volcanoes. In 79 A.D., Mount Vesuvius in Italy ❷ ______________, and the city of Pompeii was buried under ❸ ______________ for about 1,500 years. It was ❹ ______________ in 1599, and then more places in Pompeii were ❺ ______________ in 1748. Due to the lack of air and ❻ ______________, its ruins had been well preserved. So people can see how people in ❼ ______________ lived. Today, Pompeii has become one of the most ❽ ______________ places in Italy and is a UNESCO World Heritage Site.

UNIT 10 | **Subject** Art & Music **Topic** Art Museums

Let's Enjoy Art Museums!

1. Do you like to visit art museums?
2. How do you feel when you visit an art museum?

BEFORE YOU READ

A Match the words with the definitions below.

1. ______ expert
2. ______ on display
3. ______ statue
4. ______ pose (*v.*)
5. ______ allow

a. to stay in a particular position
b. to let someone do something
c. put somewhere for people to see
d. a figure of a person or animal made of stone, metal, etc.
e. a person with special knowledge of something

B Background Knowledge

Art museums are places that display artwork. The Louvre Museum in Paris, France, has Leonardo da Vinci's *Mona Lisa*. The Uffizi Gallery in Florence, Italy, features many Renaissance works of art. And the Metropolitan Museum of Art in New York City, USA, has a huge number of paintings and statues.

When people visit another country, art museums are places they often visit. However, when they visit art museums, not many people really enjoy the works of art because they have little knowledge about them. Here are several tips for enjoying art museums.

First, you do not have to be an **expert** to enjoy art. Do not try to see every piece of art **on display**. Just find some pieces you like and spend more time with them. It may be fun to guess what the artists were trying to say in their pictures. If you are with your friends, share your opinions with them.

Second, renting an audio guide is another way to enjoy art museums. It will make you understand the art much better. After listening to the audio guide, pretend to be a tour guide and explain the works of art to your friends. In addition, if you find a **statue**, pretend to be the statue and **pose** like it. That can be a lot of fun.

Knowing a lot about art makes people have more fun in art museums. However, there are still many ways to enjoy art without having much knowledge about it. So do not worry but just **allow** yourself to enjoy the art. Words 209

Q

What is the paragraph mainly about?

P1 Why people do not often (collect / enjoy) works of art

P2 (How / Where) to enjoy works of art

P3 The benefits of renting an audio guide and what you can do if you find a(n) ______________

CHECK YOUR COMPREHENSION

Choose the best answers.

Main Idea

1 **What is the passage mainly about?**

a. Ways to enjoy art museums

b. How to become an expert on art

c. What you can see in art museums

d. Why people do not enjoy art museums

Details

2 **Which is mentioned as a way to understand the art better at art museums?**

a. Finding an expert

b. Getting an audio guide

c. Asking a friend about it

d. Searching for information on the Internet

3 **Which is NOT mentioned as a way to enjoy art museums?**

a. Sharing your opinions with your friends

b. Pretending to be a tour guide for your friends

c. Trying to see as many works of art as possible

d. Guessing what artists were trying to say in their pictures

4 **What can be inferred about art museums?**

a. It is best to visit them with a tour guide.

b. Knowledge is not necessary to enjoy them.

c. You should visit them only when you are interested in art.

d. You should be an expert on art to enjoy them.

Write the answers in complete sentences.

5 **Why do many people not really enjoy the works of art at art museums?**

____

6 **What can people do when they find a statue?**

____

SHOW YOUR COMPREHENSION

Fill in the chart with the phrases from the box.

How to Enjoy Art Museums

The First Tips	• Find ❶ ________________ and spend more time with them. • Guess what the artists were trying to say in their pictures. • ❷ ________________ with your friends.
The Second Tips	• Rent an audio guide. • ❸ ________________ for your friends. • ❹ ________________ when you find one.

pose like a statue
pretend to be a tour guide
share your opinions
some pieces of art you like

SUMMARIZE YOUR READING

Complete the summary with the words from the box.

art museums　expert　audio guide　more time
say　knowledge　posing　opinions

There are several things you can do to enjoy ❶ ____________ even if you have little ❷ ____________ about art. You do not have to be a(n) ❸ ____________ to enjoy art. Choose a few pieces of art that you like and spend ❹ ____________ with them. Try to guess what the artists were trying to ❺ ____________ in their pictures and share your ❻ ____________ with your friends. You can also rent a(n) ❼ ____________ to get information about the artwork. After listening, explain the artwork to your friends like a tour guide. ❽ ____________ like a statue that you find is a lot of fun, too.

Subject Languages
Topic Idioms

I Hope You Break a Leg!

1. What is an idiom?
2. What is your favorite idiom in English and its meaning?

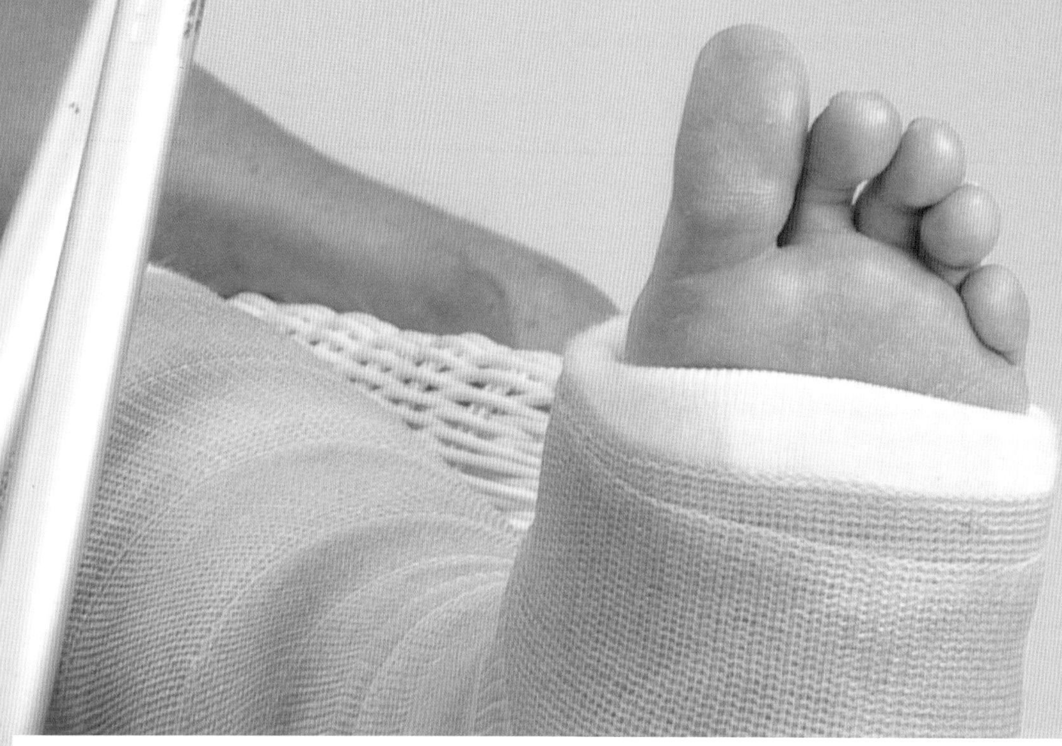

BEFORE YOU READ

A Match the words with the definitions below.

1. _____ turn (*n.*)
2. _____ confused
3. _____ superstitious
4. _____ date back to
5. _____ cheer

a. to give a loud shout
b. puzzled; unable to understand
c. believing in the power of magic or luck
d. the time when you can or must do something
e. to have started at a particular time in the past

B Background Knowledge

Idioms are words or expressions whose meanings are different from their literal meanings. For example, "a piece of cake" is an idiom meaning that something is very easy. In addition, "under the weather" means that a person feels sick. English is full of all kinds of colorful idioms.

It is your **turn** to make a presentation in front of your classmates. You feel very nervous as you walk onto the stage. Then, your teacher whispers to you, "Break a leg!" Now, you get **confused**. "Why does she want me to break my leg?" you think. She was actually wishing you good luck by saying that idiom. So where does the phrase come from? There are many possible answers.

Some say it comes from people in theaters. They often told actors to "break a leg" before they went on stage to perform. The reason was that stage actors were very **superstitious**. People thought if they said good things to actors, it would bring them bad luck. So to wish them good luck, they told actors negative expressions such as, "May you break your leg!"

Another explanation **dates back to** William Shakespeare's time. In those days, the phrase "break a leg" meant bowing by bending at the knee. When a play was excellent, the audience **cheered** the performance. Then, each actor would "break a leg" by bowing to the audience. The better the performance was, the more often the actors broke their legs. Therefore, the phrase was said to wish them success in their performances. Words 205

Q

What is the paragraph mainly about?

P1 What the idiom "________" means

P2 The (meaning / origin) of "break a leg"

P3 What "break a leg" meant during the time of ________

CHECK YOUR COMPREHENSION

Choose the best answers.

Main Idea

1 **What is the passage mainly about?**

a. Idioms that mean good luck

b. Why actors were superstitious

c. The origins of the idiom "break a leg"

d. The meanings of the idiom "break a leg"

Details

2 **According to the passage, which is NOT true about the idiom "break a leg"?**

a. It is said to wish someone good luck.

b. Its true origin is unknown.

c. It was often said in theaters.

d. It comes from one of Shakespeare's plays.

3 **Today, the idiom "break a leg" can be said ____________________.**

a. to nobody

b. only to actors

c. to actors and other people

d. only to actors and musicians

4 **Which is NOT a situation where you can say, "Break a leg"?**

a. Kevin falls off his bike and breaks his leg.

b. Ann is waiting for her turn to give a speech.

c. Mike is practicing for an audition tomorrow.

d. Jane is about to take part in a dance contest.

Write the answers in complete sentences.

5 **Why did people tell actors negative expressions before their performances?**

____

6 **What was the original meaning of "break a leg" in William Shakespeare's time?**

____

SHOW YOUR COMPREHENSION

Fill in the chart with the phrases from the box.

"Break a Leg!"

People in Theaters	• They thought ❶ ______________ to actors would bring them bad luck. • They told actors ❷ ______________ to wish them good luck.
In William Shakespeare's Time	• It meant bowing ❸ ______________. • As an audience cheered, the actors "broke their legs" more often. • The phrase was said to ❹ ______________ in their performances.

wish actors success
negative expressions
saying good things
by bending at the knee

SUMMARIZE YOUR READING

Complete the summary with the words from the box.

theaters superstitious good luck perform well
bowing origin bad luck cheered

To wish someone good luck, we may say, "Break a leg." There are many stories about the ❶ ______________ of the idiom. Some say it was from people in ❷ ______________. Actors were ❸ ______________. They believed saying good words to actors would bring them ❹ ______________. So they said negative expressions to wish them ❺ ______________. Others say the phrase referred to bowing by bending at the knee in Shakespeare's time. When actors performed well, the audience ❻ ______________. Then, the actors would "break their legs" by ❼ ______________ to the audience. So when people said, "Break a leg," they hoped the actors would ❽ ______________.

UNIT 12 | Subject Earth Science
Topic Space Tourism

Traveling in Space

1. Would you like to go into space?
2. What would it be like to go into space?

BEFORE YOU READ

A Match the words with the definitions below.

1. ______ outer space
2. ______ space agency
3. ______ spacecraft
4. ______ surface
5. ______ ambitious

a. a vehicle that can travel in space
b. the outer or top part of something
c. the area beyond the Earth's atmosphere
d. strongly wanting to be successful in some way
e. an organization that sends people or machines into space

B Background Knowledge

The Russian astronaut Yuri Gagarin was the first person to go to outer space in 1961. After that, hundreds of people visited space for their countries' space agencies. Then, in 2001, Dennis Tito, an American businessman, paid 20 million dollars and became the first space tourist. He spent nearly eight days at the International Space Station. Today, several companies have plans to take tourists into space.

In 1961, Yuri Gagarin became the first man in **outer space**. Since then, more than 500 people have gone into space. Most worked for their countries' **space agencies**. Just a few were tourists.

Millions of people have dreamed of traveling into space since they first looked up at the night sky. This is about to become reality for some of them. This is mostly due to three men: Richard Branson, Jeff Bezos, and Elon Musk. In July 2021, Branson, the owner of Virgin Galactic, went into space on the *VSS Unity*, his company's **spacecraft**. Days later, Jeff Bezos, the founder of Amazon.com and the owner of Blue Origin, visited space, too. Their trips were short. But they showed that their companies were ready to take tourists into space.

Virgin Galactic and Blue Origin will fly into *suborbital space. That is more than eighty kilometers above the Earth's **surface**. Elon Musk's company, SpaceX, is more **ambitious**. It will fly tourists into *orbital space and even to the International Space Station.

These flights are not cheap. The least expensive one costs $200,000. But as more flights go into space, prices will go down. Soon, going into space may be almost as cheap as flying across an ocean. Words 205

* **suborbital space** the first layer of space where spacecraft cannot orbit the Earth

* **orbital space** the second layer of space where spacecraft have escaped the Earth's gravity

What is the paragraph mainly about?

P1 What kind of people have visited ______

P2 The companies of (three / four) men and their efforts to go to space

P3 Which parts of space each ______ will fly to

P4 (How much / How long) a flight into space will be

▲The Virgin Galactic spacecraft

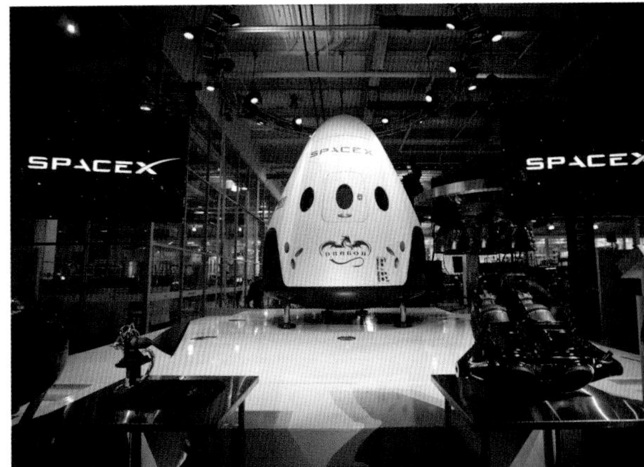

▲The SpaceX spacecraft

CHECK YOUR COMPREHENSION

Choose the best answers.

Main Idea

1 **What is the passage mainly about?**

a. Virgin Galactic and SpaceX
b. The International Space Station
c. The companies of three rich men
d. Efforts to take tourists into space

Details

2 **According to the passage, which is true about Richard Branson?**

a. He is the founder of Amazon.com.
b. He has not visited outer space yet.
c. He flew on the spacecraft *VSS Unity*.
d. He is working together with Elon Musk.

3 ______________ **will fly tourists into orbital space.**

a. SpaceX
b. *VSS Unity*
c. Virgin Galactic
d. Blue Origin

4 **What can be inferred from the passage?**

a. SpaceX has plans to build a space station.
b. Richard Branson's company is the most successful.
c. Only rich people will go into outer space at first.
d. Jeff Bezos has no plans to visit outer space.

Write the answers in complete sentences.

5 **What did Richard Branson and Jeff Bezos show people?**

____

6 **How much does a flight into outer space cost?**

____

SHOW YOUR COMPREHENSION

Fill in the chart with the phrases from the box.

Space Tourism

Richard Branson	• is the owner of Virgin Galactic • flew into outer space ❶ ____________ • will ❷ ____________
Jeff Bezos	• is the founder of Amazon.com and the owner of Blue Origin • flew into outer space ❸ ____________ • will fly tourists to suborbital space
Elon Musk	• owns the company SpaceX • has ambitious plans to fly to ❹ ____________ • will fly tourists into orbital space

on the *VSS Unity* in July 2021
fly tourists to suborbital space
the International Space Station
a few days after Richard Branson

SUMMARIZE YOUR READING

Complete the summary with the words from the box.

Jeff Bezos | first man | *VSS Unity* | orbital space
space | go down | suborbital space | tourists

Yuri Gagarin was the ❶ ____________ to visit outer space in 1961. Only a few people after him were ❷ ____________. However, this will change soon. Richard Branson, ❸ ____________, and Elon Musk have companies that will take tourists into ❹ ____________. Richard Branson visited space on the ❺ ____________ in July 2021. Jeff Bezos, the owner of Blue Origin, also flew into space. Their companies will visit ❻ ____________. Elon Musk's company, SpaceX, will fly tourists to ❼ ____________ and to the International Space Station. Flights will cost at least $200,000, but the prices will ❽ ____________ later.

THINK & WRITE 3

Are You For or Against Space Tourism?

STEP 1 DISCUSSION **Talk to your partner and answer the questions.**

1. Do you think space tourism is a good or bad thing?
2. Why do some people want to go into space?

STEP 2 ORGANIZATION **Fill in the chart with the phrases from the box.**

engineers will start building	encourage others to go there
will be able to go to space soon	in places other than the planet Earth
will travel faster and farther	people living on the moon and Mars

Introduction	I am in favor of space tourism.
Body	**Supporting sentence 1:** More people ____________________. **Details:** Those people will promote space and ____________________. **Supporting sentence 2:** With more people in space, ____________________ better spaceships. **Details:** These ships ____________________ than current ships can go. **Supporting sentence 3:** Space tourism will eventually lead to ____________________. **Details:** Humans will be able to live ____________________.
Conclusion	Thanks to space tourism, people will promote space, engineers will make better spaceships, and people will live on the moon and Mars.

STEP 3 FIRST DRAFT **Complete the writing with the phrases from the chart.**

Title Are You For or Against Space Tourism?

I am in favor of space tourism.

First, more people ______________________. Those people will promote space and ______________________.

Second, with more people in space, ______________________ better spaceships. These ships ______________________ than current ships can go.

Lastly, space tourism will eventually lead to ______________________. Humans will be able to live ______________________.

Thanks to space tourism, people will promote space, engineers will make better spaceships, and people will live on the moon and Mars.

STEP 4 FINAL DRAFT **Complete the writing. Replace one of the details with you own idea.**

Title ______________________

I am in favor of space tourism.

First, ______________________

____

Second, ______________________

____

Finally, ______________________

____

Thanks to space tourism, ______________________

____

CHAPTER 04

UNIT 13 | **Subject** Social Studies **Topic** Murphy's Law

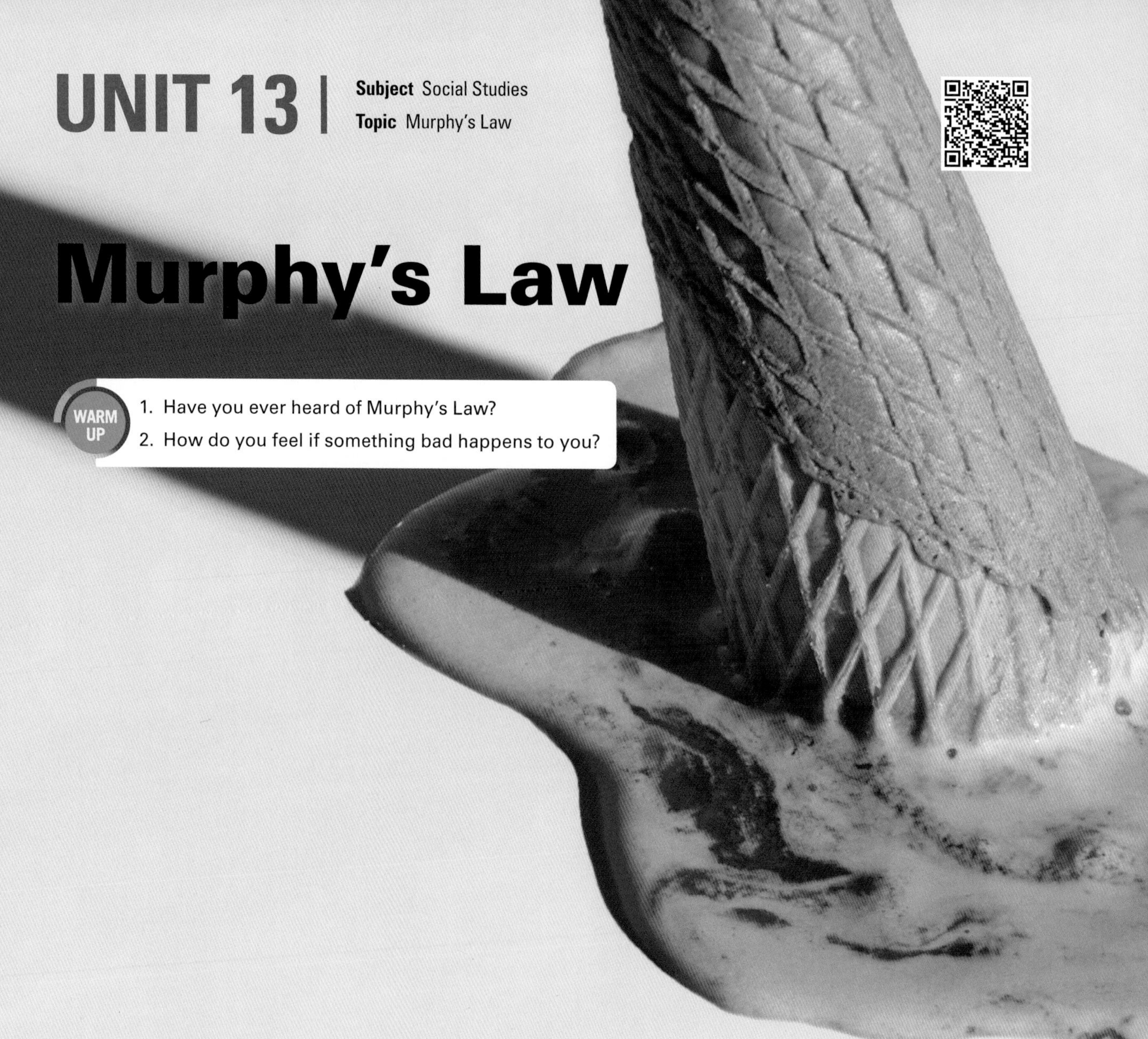

Murphy's Law

WARM UP
1. Have you ever heard of Murphy's Law?
2. How do you feel if something bad happens to you?

BEFORE YOU READ

A Match the words with the definitions below.

1. ______ go wrong
2. ______ much-awaited
3. ______ coin (*v.*)
4. ______ carry out
5. ______ injury

a. highly expected
b. to turn out badly
c. damage done to a person's body
d. to invent a new word or expression
e. to do a particular piece of work, research, etc.

B Background Knowledge

When something can go wrong, it will go wrong. That is basically Murphy's Law. However, you have probably experienced a time when everything went right for you. Perhaps you were extremely lucky for some reason. When things go perfectly, that is an example of Sally's Law.

Murphy's Law is not something that law school students need to know. The expression is often used to mean "If anything can **go wrong**, it will."

There are plenty of examples of Murphy's Law around us. For example, when you change lines at a store, the other lines always move faster. Then, you regret changing lines. In another case, on your **much-awaited** picnic day, it suddenly starts raining. In that case, you might start screaming, "Why me? Why today?"

Although it is not clear who first **coined** the expression, there are two different views on Murphy's Law. It was named after Edward A. Murphy, a U.S. Air Force engineer. One day, he was **carrying out** an important test. It failed because one assistant made a mistake. There were no bad **injuries** though. Not happy with the failure, Murphy said about the assistant, "If there is any way to make a mistake, he will."

Later, however, USAF *Colonel John Paul Stapp focused on the bright side of the same situation. He said, "We always thought about Murphy's Law that things can go wrong. So we prepared more and had no big injuries during the tests." Words 194

* **colonel** an officer of high rank in the army, the marines, or the air force

Q

What is the paragraph mainly about?

P1 What ______________ is

P2 Some ______________ of Murphy's Law

P3 The (origin / result) of Murphy's Law

P4 Another (name / view) of Murphy's Law

CHECK YOUR COMPREHENSION

Choose the best answers.

Main Idea

1 **What is the passage mainly about?**

a. Laws people should know

b. Why some people are unlucky

c. Different views on Murphy's Law

d. Who coined the term Murphy's Law

Details

2 **According to the passage, which is NOT true about Edward A. Murphy?**

a. He made the term Murphy's Law.

b. He was an engineer in the U.S. Air Force.

c. He blamed his assistant for a mistake.

d. He looked on the dark side of things.

3 **John Paul Stapp tried to be positive about the situation because ______________.**

a. the test finally succeeded

b. no one was seriously hurt

c. anyone can make mistakes

d. a mistake was not discovered

4 **Which is NOT an example of Murphy's Law?**

a. It rains when you wash your car.

b. The item you want to buy is not on sale.

c. When you are in the bathtub, the doorbell rings.

d. When you do not do your homework, the teacher forgets to check it.

Write the answers in complete sentences.

5 **What did Edward A. Murphy say about his assistant?**

____

6 **What two examples of Murphy's Law are introduced in the passage?**

____

SHOW YOUR COMPREHENSION

Fill in the chart with the phrases from the box.

Murphy's Law

Meaning	• It is the idea that ❶ ____________________.
Examples	• You wait longer if you ❷ ____________________. • It starts raining on your much-awaited picnic day.
Different Views on Murphy's Law	• Edward A. Murphy - focused on ❸ ____________________ • John Paul Stapp - thought that they ❹ ____________________ and had no big injuries

change lines at a store
his assistant's mistake
could prepare more
if anything can go wrong, it will

SUMMARIZE YOUR READING

Complete the summary with the words from the box.

coined　unhappy　different views　big injuries
mistake　bright side　go wrong　prepare

Murphy's Law is the idea that if anything can ❶ __________, it will. We experience many examples of it. It is unknown who ❷ __________ the expression, but there are two ❸ __________ on it. An assistant in the U.S. Air Force made a mistake during a test, so the test failed. One person felt ❹ __________ about the failure and focused on the assistant's ❺ __________. On the other hand, another person focused on the ❻ __________ of the same situation. He said that because of Murphy's Law, they could ❼ __________ more and prevent ❽ __________.

UNIT 14 | Subject Life Science / Topic Animal Senses

Can Animals Predict Natural Disasters?

WARM UP

1. What special senses do animals have?
2. Do you think animals can predict natural disasters?

BEFORE YOU READ

A Match the words with the definitions below.

1. ______ in a panic		a. to find or locate
2. ______ hibernate		b. afraid; full of fear
3. ______ tremor		c. a small earthquake
4. ______ detect		d. outstanding; impressive
5. ______ exceptional		e. to sleep for a long time, often in winter

B Background Knowledge

Many animals have senses stronger than those of humans. For example, dogs and cats can hear sounds much higher than humans can. Their sense of smell is very strong, too. Bees can see colors than humans cannot. And ants are able to detect movement through dirt.

Dogs on the streets begin to bark loudly. Some run around **in a panic**. They seem scared. A few minutes later, an earthquake strikes. Did the dogs know it was coming?

Q

What is the paragraph mainly about?

P2 How animals acted before ______________ took place

This happened in Gujarat, India, in 2001. A powerful earthquake struck the area and caused a lot of damage. And right before it took place, the dogs nearby went crazy. Similar events have occurred in other places. In 2012, goats on Mount Etna in Sicily ran off the mountain. Several hours later, the volcano erupted. In February 1975, **hibernating** snakes in Haicheng, China, departed their burrows. A bit later, an earthquake hit the city. Scientists have observed other animals acting strangely before natural disasters. These include toads, ants, ducks, and flamingos.

How can these animals tell trouble is coming? Scientists have some theories. One is that animals can sense **tremors** in the ground. Other animals can **detect** changes in air pressure. That tells them a hurricane or typhoon is coming. And some animals, such as dogs, have **exceptional** hearing. This lets them know about natural disasters, too.

P3 Theories on (how / where) animals can tell trouble is coming

Can animals predict natural disasters? It seems possible. So if your dog starts acting strangely for no reason, be careful.

Words 198

CHECK YOUR COMPREHENSION

Choose the best answers.

Main Idea

1 **What is the passage mainly about?**

a. The most famous natural disasters in history

b. Natural disasters that have killed many animals

c. How natural disasters sometimes affect animals

d. The ability of animals to know about natural disasters

Details

2 **What did some goats seem to predict in 2012?**

a. A tsunami

b. An earthquake

c. A hurricane

d. A volcanic eruption

3 **Scientists believe that some animals can ________________.**

a. hear thunderstorms coming

b. feel the temperature getting colder

c. know when the air pressure changes

d. smell changes in the air

4 **What can be inferred from the passage?**

a. Natural disasters happen very often.

b. Most natural disasters are not dangerous.

c. Animals are not afraid of natural disasters.

d. Some animals have better senses than people.

Write the answers in complete sentences.

5 **What happened before an earthquake hit Gujarat, India, in 2001?**

____

6 **How did some snakes act strangely in Haicheng, China, in 1975?**

____

SHOW YOUR COMPREHENSION

Fill in the chart with the phrases from the box.

Animals and Natural Disasters

What Animals Did Before Natural Disasters	• Some dogs went crazy before a powerful earthquake struck Gujarat, India. • Goats on Mount Etna ❶ ______________ before the volcano erupted. • Hibernating snakes ❷ ______________ in Haicheng, China, before an earthquake hit.
What Scientists Believe	• Animals ❸ ______________ in the ground. • Some animals can detect changes in air pressure. • Animals like dogs ❹ ______________.

can sense tremors
departed their burrow
have exceptional hearing
ran off the mountain

SUMMARIZE YOUR READING

Complete the summary with the words from the box.

exceptional natural disasters volcano hibernating
tremors theories changes acting strangely

Some dogs went crazy before an earthquake in Gujarat, India, in 2001. Goats on Mount Etna ran off the mountain in 2012. Later, the ❶ ______________ erupted. In 1975, ❷ ______________ snakes left their burrows in Haicheng, China. Then, an earthquake happened. Animals like toads, ants, ducks, and flamingos have been observed ❸ ______________ before natural disasters happened. Some scientists have ❹ ______________ on how animals seem to know about natural disasters. Some think animals can detect ❺ ______________ in the ground and ❻ ______________ in air pressure. Other animals, like dogs, have ❼ ______________ hearing. These abilities let animals know when ❽ ______________ are coming.

UNIT 15 | Subject Art & Music
Topic Masks

A False Face

WARM UP
1. What kinds of masks are there in your country?
2. Why do people wear masks?

BEFORE YOU READ

A Match the words with the definitions below.

1. ______ disguise (*n.*) a. a soul
2. ______ ritual b. to laugh at
3. ______ mock c. to be a symbol of something
4. ______ represent d. the act of changing how you look
5. ______ spirit e. done as part of a religious ceremony

B Background Knowledge

Masks are objects that cover the face. The oldest mask ever found is more than 9,000 years old. People have made masks with wood, leather, metal, and other materials. They have used masks for religious ceremonies, parties, plays, wars, fashion, and many other reasons.

You may have watched a program on TV in which African people wearing masks were dancing in a ceremony. Masks differ from country to country and have been used for various reasons. Some have been used for **disguises** or performances. Others have been used for ceremonies and **ritual** reasons.

During the time of the Republic of Venice, there were very strict class differences. Therefore, wearing masks gave people the chance to hide which class they were in. In Korea, people used masks in traditional dances. They would take great joy in **mocking** the ruling class through mask dances. In Chinese operas, masks **represent** the personality of each character by using different colors. That way, audiences can easily imagine what the characters are like.

In ancient Egypt, people made death masks. They were put on dead people's faces. The Egyptians believed each mask could help a soul recognize its body and return to it. In Africa, animal masks symbolize the **spirits** of animals. The masks are thought to help the wearers become the animals themselves and communicate with the animals.

It is interesting to know how masks have been used in different countries. It seems that masks have one thing in common: They all cover people's faces. Words 206

Q

What is the paragraph mainly about?

P1 Why people have used ______________ in different countries

P2 When people wear masks for (disguises or performances / ceremonies and ritual reasons)

P3 When people wear masks for (disguises or performances / ceremonies and ritual reasons)

P4 What masks have in ______________

▲The golden mask of Tutankhamun

CHECK YOUR COMPREHENSION

Choose the best answers.

Main Idea

1 **What is the passage mainly about?**

a. How masks have changed over time

b. The uses of masks in different countries

c. The reason why people wore masks in the past

d. The common features of masks around the world

Details

2 **Why did people wear masks during the time of the Republic of Venice?**

a. They wanted to protect their faces.

b. They wanted to look more attractive.

c. They wanted to hide their social classes.

d. They wanted to express their personalities.

3 ______________ **were most likely the audience for Korean mask dances.**

a. Kings

b. Children

c. Noblemen

d. Ordinary people

4 **What can be inferred from the passage?**

a. In the Republic of Venice, only people in the lower classes wore masks.

b. Korean people in the past had no complaints about their rulers.

c. The ancient Egyptians did not believe in life after death.

d. African people believe that animals have souls like humans.

Write the answers in complete sentences.

5 **Why do masks used in Chinese operas have different colors?**

____

6 **Why did the Egyptians put masks on dead people's faces?**

____

SHOW YOUR COMPREHENSION

Fill in the chart with the phrases from the box.

Masks

For Disguises or Performances	• During the time for the Republic of Venice, masks were used to ❶ ______________. • In Korea, people used masks in traditional dances to ❷ ______________. • In Chinese operas, masks represent each character's personality.
For Ceremonies and Ritual Reasons	• Egyptian death masks were believed to help a dead person's soul ❸ ______________. • African animal masks are thought to help the wearers ❹ ______________.

return to its body
hide people's classes
mock the ruling class
communicate with the animals

SUMMARIZE YOUR READING

Complete the summary with the words from the box.

dead person　color　differences　recognize
animals　uses　spirits　mask dances

Masks have had a variety of ❶ ______________ from country to country. During the time of the Republic of Venice, people wore masks to hide their class ❷ ______________. In Korea, people would mock the ruling class through ❸ ______________. In Chinese operas, the ❹ ______________ of an actor's mask shows the character's personality. Ancient Egyptians placed a mask on the face of a(n) ❺ ______________. People then believed that the soul could ❻ ______________ its body and come back to it. In Africa, animal masks are thought to help the wearers connect with the ❼ ______________ because the masks symbolize the ❽ ______________ of the animals.

UNIT 16 | **Subject** History **Topic** The Fortune Cookie

Show Me My Fortune

1. Have you ever had a fortune cookie?
2. Where do you think fortune cookies originated?

BEFORE YOU READ

A Match the words with the definitions below.

1. ______ split a. finally; eventually
2. ______ previous b. to make something popular
3. ______ immigrant c. to divide into two or more parts
4. ______ popularize d. earlier; past
5. ______ ultimately e. a person who comes to live permanently in a foreign country

B Background Knowledge

There are special desserts everywhere. Gelato is a soft ice cream made in Italy. It comes in many flavors. Belgian waffles are popular in Belgium. People eat them with powdered sugar or ice cream on top. In Egypt, people enjoy *om ali*, a kind of bread pudding with raisins and nuts.

Imagine that you are served a cookie for dessert after you eat a meal. When you **split** the cookie into two, there is a piece of paper inside with a message or a list of lucky numbers. The message on the paper tells you your fortune. We call this cookie a fortune cookie.

Fortune cookies are made from flour, sugar, vanilla, and sesame seed oil, and a piece of "fortune" paper is inside. People enjoy them because it is fun to read the messages on the paper. In addition, the lists of lucky numbers contain **previous** winning lottery numbers.

Chinese restaurants in the United States often serve fortune cookies for dessert. Although you may think that they are from China, there are no fortune cookies in China. They are based on **omikuji*, which was used in Japanese temples in the 19th century.

▲ *Omikuji*

In the early 20th century, Japanese **immigrants** to California introduced fortune cookies to the United States. Then, they were **popularized** by Chinese restaurants there. There is a saying, "Fortune cookies were introduced by the Japanese, popularized by the Chinese, but **ultimately** eaten by the Americans." The next time you visit a Chinese restaurant, find out your fortune. Words 199

* ***omikuji*** a strip of paper on which one's fortune is written

Q

What is the paragraph mainly about?

P1 What a(n) ______________ is

P2 What fortune cookies (are made from / taste like) and what is inside them

P3 The (popularity / origin) of the fortune cookie

P4 How fortune cookies were introduced to the U.S. and ______________

An adventure is coming up.

CHECK YOUR COMPREHENSION

Choose the best answers.

Main Idea

1 **What is the passage mainly about?**

a. How to make fortune cookies

b. The history of fortune cookies

c. Who invented the fortune cookie

d. The popularity of fortune cookies

Details

2 **Which is mentioned as a reason people like fortune cookies?**

a. They are delicious.

b. They are easy to make.

c. People believe that they bring good luck.

d. People like to read the messages inside them.

3 **Fortune cookies are originally from _______________.**

a. China

b. Japan

c. the United States

d. a Chinese restaurant

4 **What can be inferred about fortune cookies?**

a. They are not Chinese food.

b. They are eaten on special days.

c. They were first made by an American.

d. The messages in the cookies are written in Chinese.

Write the answers in complete sentences.

5 **Who introduced fortune cookies to the United States?**

____

6 **How did fortune cookies become popular in the United States?**

____

SHOW YOUR COMPREHENSION

Fill in the chart with the phrases from the box.

The Fortune Cookie

What the Fortune Cookie Is	• is ❶ ______________ or a list of lucky numbers inside
Where Fortune Cookies Come From	• are ❷ ______________, which was used in Japanese temples
How They Became Popular	• were introduced to the U.S. by ❸ ______________ to California • were popularized by ❹ ______________

based on *omikuji*
a cookie with a message
Chinese restaurants in the U.S.
Japanese immigrants

SUMMARIZE YOUR READING

Complete the summary with the words from the box.

fortune Japanese temples introduced Americans
come from popular lucky numbers split

Fortune cookies are often served in Chinese restaurants in the U.S. When people ❶ ______________ the cookie into two, they find a piece of paper with a(n) ❷ ______________ or a list of ❸ ______________ written on it. Although many people enjoy them, they might not know where the cookies ❹ ______________. They originated from ❺ ______________. In the early 20th century, the cookies were ❻ ______________ to the United States by Japanese people living in California. Then, the cookies became ❼ ______________ thanks to Chinese restaurants in the U.S. As a result, the cookies are enjoyed by a lot of ❽ ______________ today.

THINK & WRITE 4

What Are Some Foods Koreans Have for Special Occasions?

STEP 1 DISCUSSION **Talk to your partner and answer the questions.**

1. What special foods do some Koreans eat?
2. When do Koreans eat those special foods?

STEP 2 ORGANIZATION **Fill in the chart with the phrases from the box.**

have seaweed soup	they will get one year older
have rice cake soup	is also a nutritious meal
a half-moon shaped rice cake	enjoy eating *songpyeon*

Introduction	Koreans eat lots of foods on special occasions.
Body	**Supporting sentence 1:** On New Year's Day, Koreans usually ______________________. **Details:** Koreans believe that if they eat a bowl of it, ______________________. **Supporting sentence 2:** Koreans also ______________________ during Chuseok. **Details:** It is ______________________ filled with sweet things. **Supporting sentence 3:** On their birthdays, many Koreans ______________________. **Details:** It tastes good, and it ______________________.
Conclusion	Koreans often enjoy rice cake soup on New Year's Day, *songpyeon* during Chuseok, and seaweed soup on their birthdays.

STEP 3 FIRST DRAFT **Complete the writing with the phrases from the chart.**

Title What Are Some Foods Koreans Have for Special Occasions?

Koreans eat lots of foods on special occasions.

First, on New Year's Day, Koreans usually ______________________. Koreans believe that if they eat a bowl of it, ______________________.

Second, Koreans also ______________________ during Chuseok. It is ______________________ filled with sweet things.

Lastly, on their birthdays, many Koreans ______________________. It tastes good, and it ______________________.

Koreans often enjoy rice cake soup on New Year's Day, *songpyeon* during Chuseok, and seaweed soup on their birthdays.

STEP 4 FINAL DRAFT **Complete the writing. Replace one of the details with you own idea.**

Title ______________________

Koreans eat lots of foods on special occasions.

First, ______________________

____

Second, ______________________

____

Lastly, ______________________

____

Koreans often enjoy ______________________

____

CHAPTER
05

UNIT 17 | Subject Language Topic Body Language

Actions Speak Louder Than Words

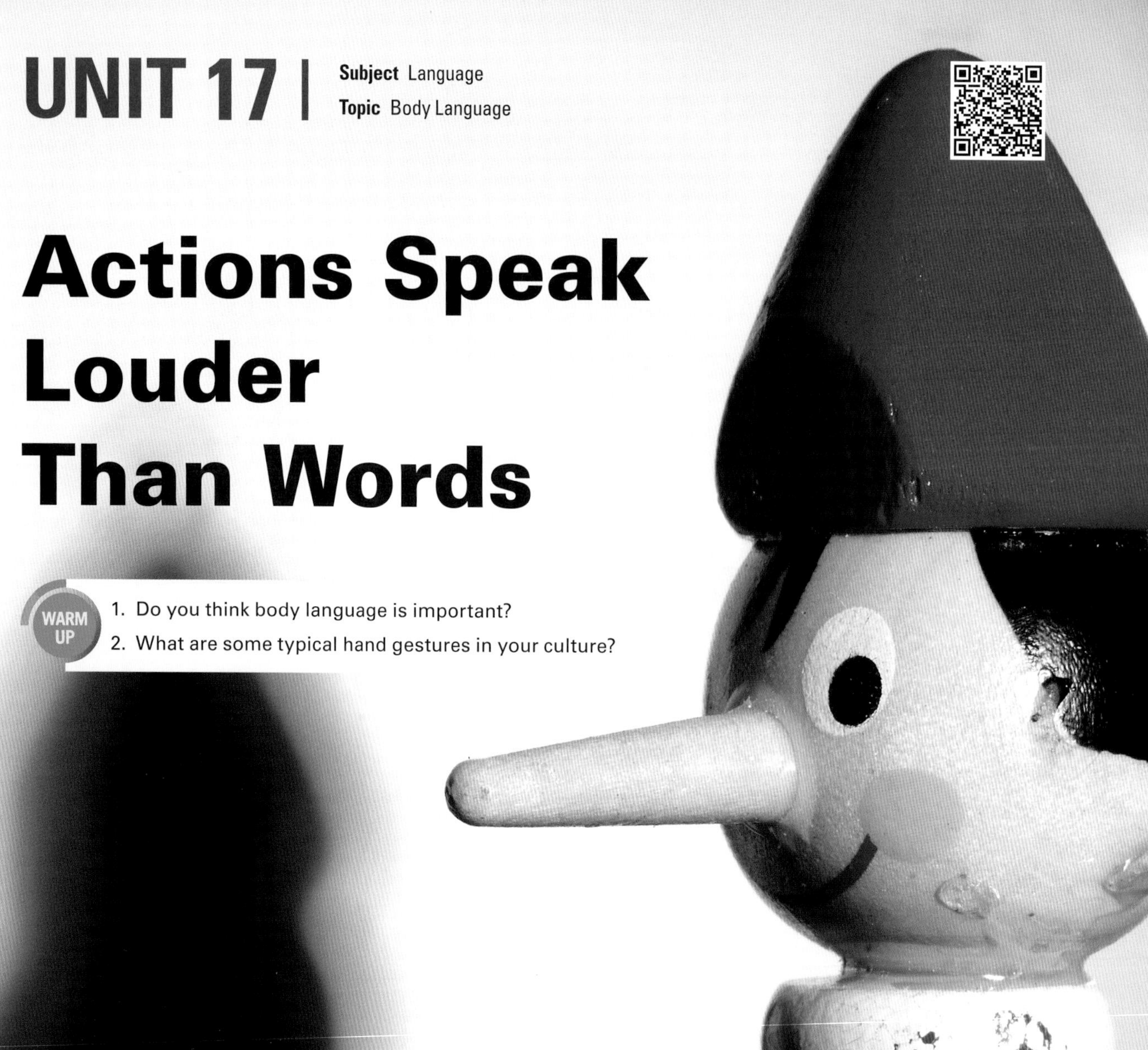

WARM UP
1. Do you think body language is important?
2. What are some typical hand gestures in your culture?

BEFORE YOU READ

A Match the words with the definitions below.

1. ______ prove
2. ______ means (*n.*)
3. ______ anxious
4. ______ unwilling
5. ______ steeple

a. nervous; worried
b. not wanting to do something
c. to show that something is true
d. a tall, pointed tower on a church
e. a method or way of doing something

B Background Knowledge

People can use body language to communicate. It involves using body parts, such as the hands, arms, and face, to say something. For instance, nodding one's head means "yes" in most cultures. Shrugging one's shoulders means "I don't know." Body language, especially facial expressions, often shows how a person feels.

"Mom, I didn't do it. While you were out, a monster came through the window and messed up the room." You are telling a lie to your mom. Certainly, your nose is not growing like Pinocchio's. But do you know what? Your body is telling the truth.

Researchers from the University of Granada in Spain studied body language. They **proved** that your nose gets warm when you tell a lie. It is called the Pinocchio Effect. Humans understand each other through language. However, it is not the only **means** of communication. We also use our bodies to make ourselves understood. So there is a saying "Actions speak louder than words."

As for the other parts of your body, your hands say a lot. For example, covering your mouth with a hand may mean you are hiding something. When you tell a lie, you feel **anxious**. So you cover your mouth to stop yourself from telling more lies. Putting your hands in your pockets may mean you are **unwilling** to do something. So what do your hands show with the following gesture? You join your fingers to make a church **steeple**. This hand gesture shows that you are confident. Words 198

Q

What is the paragraph mainly about?

P2 The ______________ and how humans communicate with their bodies

P3 What different actions with your (face / hands) mean

CHECK YOUR COMPREHENSION

Choose the best answers.

Main Idea

1 **What is the passage mainly about?**

a. What the Pinocchio Effect is

b. What body language tells us

c. How to tell if someone is lying

d. Hand gestures and their meanings

Details

2 **What does the Pinocchio Effect mean?**

a. Children tell lies more often than adults.

b. People tell lies more when they feel nervous.

c. When people tell lies, their noses become warm.

d. When people tell lies, their noses actually grow longer.

3 **According to the passage, putting your hands in your pockets may mean ______________________.**

a. you feel bored

b. you feel confident

c. you are telling a lie

d. you do not want to do something

4 **According to the passage, how can you tell if someone is lying?**

a. By reading that person's lips

b. By watching that person closely

c. By asking that person a lot of questions

d. By listening carefully to what that person says

Write the answers in complete sentences.

5 **Why do people cover their mouth when they tell a lie?**

____

6 **What does it mean when a man joins his fingers to make a church steeple?**

____

SHOW YOUR COMPREHENSION

Fill in the chart with the phrases from the box.

Body Language

The Pinocchio Effect	• When you tell a lie, ❶ ______________. • It shows that your body is ❷ ______________.
Examples of Hand Gestures	• Covering the mouth - You are hiding something. • Putting your hands in your pockets - You are ❸ ______________. • Joining your fingers to ❹ ______________ - You are confident.

make a church steeple
unwilling to do something
your nose gets warm
another means of communication

SUMMARIZE YOUR READING

Complete the summary with the words from the box.

Pinocchio Effect hands pockets mouth
grows confidence bodies gets warm

When Pinocchio tells a lie, his nose ❶ ______________. Similarly, our ❷ ______________ may show the truth as well. For example, there is the ❸ ______________. When you tell a lie, your nose ❹ ______________. In addition, your ❺ ______________ speak a lot. Putting your hand over your ❻ ______________ may mean you are hiding something and do not want to tell any more lies. Having your hands in your ❼ ______________ may mean an unwillingness to do something. How about putting your fingertips together like a church steeple? It may show your ❽ ______________.

UNIT 18 | **Subject** Life Science **Topic** Epidemics and Pandemics

Disease Outbreaks

WARM UP
1. What are some infectious diseases?
2. What are some of the worst diseases in history?

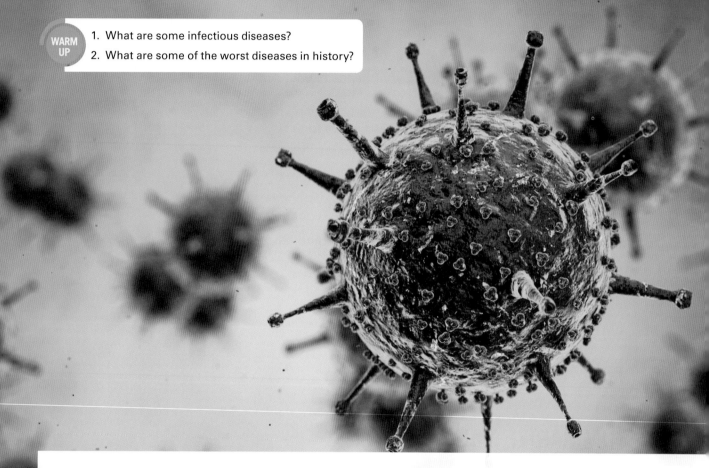

BEFORE YOU READ

A Match the words with the definitions below.

1. ______ disease a. many in number
2. ______ infect b. an illness
3. ______ outbreak c. not one nor the other of two things or people
4. ______ multiple d. to make a person sick
5. ______ neither e. the sudden occurrence of something bad

B Background Knowledge

Viruses are made up of genetic material (DNA or RNA) and a protein coat. They inject genetic material into cells and reproduce. This makes people get sick. Infectious viruses like the flu, chicken pox, and measles can move from one person to another. Vaccines can protect people from some viruses.

In late 2019, a new **disease** appeared in Asia. Soon, the virus spread rapidly around the world. Called COVID-19, by mid-2021, it **infected** nearly 200 million people. It also killed more than four million people. Due to its global effects, COVID-19 was called a pandemic.

Q

What is the paragraph mainly about?

P1 How ________ became a pandemic

Before a disease becomes a pandemic, it is an epidemic. An epidemic is an **outbreak** of a disease that spreads quickly in a limited area. It may be a community, a city, or a country. Some, like the *smallpox epidemic in Mexico in 1520, kill millions of people. Others infect many people but do not kill large numbers of them. Instead, perhaps only thousands of people die.

P2 What (a pandemic / an epidemic) is

When an epidemic spreads more widely, it becomes a pandemic. A pandemic may affect **multiple** countries or even the entire world. In the 1300s, the Black Death spread from Asia to Europe. When it ended, up to half of Europe's population was dead. In 1918, the Spanish flu spread around the world. It killed up to 100 million people in three years. Other pandemics made many people sick but killed smaller numbers of them.

▲The Black Death in Europe

P3 Some deadly ________ from the past

Not all epidemics become pandemics. And **neither** always kills millions of people. But pandemics do spread widely and infect many people. Words 207

P4 Some (examples / characteristics) of epidemics and pandemics

* **smallpox** a highly contagious disease that leaves scars on its victims' bodies

CHECK YOUR COMPREHENSION

Choose the best answers.

Main Idea

1 **What is the passage mainly about?**

a. Where COVID-19 comes from

b. The worst pandemics in history

c. How viruses spread to other people

d. What epidemics and pandemics are

Details

2 **According to the passage, what happened in 1520?**

a. Millions of Mexicans died because of smallpox.

b. The Black Death spread through much of Europe.

c. The Spanish flu killed up to 100 million people.

d. More than 200 million people died in a pandemic.

3 **Millions of people died starting in 1918 because of ____________.**

a. smallpox

b. COVID-19

c. the Spanish flu

d. the Black Death

4 **What can be inferred from the passage?**

a. Doctors are not able to stop pandemics.

b. Epidemics affect more people than pandemics.

c. The Spanish flu mostly killed people in Europe.

d. The Black Death occurred in more than two continents.

Write the answers in complete sentences.

5 **What is an epidemic?**

____

6 **When does an epidemic become a pandemic?**

____

SHOW YOUR COMPREHENSION

Fill in the chart with the phrases from the box.

Epidemics and Pandemics

Epidemics	• are outbreaks of diseases that spread quickly ❶ ________ • happened in 1520 in Mexico, where millions of people died • may kill millions of people or ❷ ________ but not kill many of them
Pandemics	• occur when epidemics ❸ ________ • may ❹ ________ or the entire world • include COVID-19, the Black Death, and the Spanish flu

affect multiple countries
in limited areas
infect a lot of people
spread more widely

SUMMARIZE YOUR READING

Complete the summary with the words from the box.

pandemic kill entire world Spanish flu
spread COVID-19 sick outbreak

❶ ________ appeared in Asia in late 2019 and ❷ ________ around the world. By mid-2021, it was a(n) ❸ ________ that killed more than four million people. An epidemic is a(n) ❹ ________ of a disease in a limited area, but a pandemic spreads to many countries or the ❺ ________. Both of them can ❻ ________ millions of people. An epidemic in Mexico in 1520 killed millions. The Black Death and the ❼ ________ were deadly pandemics. They both killed large numbers of people. Other epidemics and pandemics made people ❽ ________ but did not kill many of them.

The Bravest Girl in the World

WARM UP

1. Who is the bravest person you know?
2. Have you ever been brave? What did you do?

BEFORE YOU READ

A Match the words with the definitions below.

1. _____ cruelty
2. _____ treatment
3. _____ outraged
4. _____ critical
5. _____ nominate

a. seriously ill
b. extremely angry
c. medical care given to a sick person
d. an action that causes pain to a person or animal
e. officially to suggest someone for a job, position, or prize

B Background Knowledge

Malala Yousafzai won the Nobel Peace Prize in 2014. She became the youngest winner ever at the age of 17. Since then, she has received many other prizes. She also works as an activist for the rights of girls and women.

On October 9, 2012, a girl in Pakistan got shot in the head and the neck on a school bus by the Taliban. This news shocked people around the world, and they wanted to know more about who she was and why she got shot.

Malala Yousafzai was born on July 12, 1997, in the Swat Valley in Pakistan. In the Swat Valley, the Taliban had stopped girls from attending school. In 2009, at the age of 12, Malala wrote a blog for the BBC about the Taliban's **cruelty**. The blog soon became famous worldwide. However, it made the Taliban upset, and they shot her while she was returning home on a school bus. She nearly died, and she was moved to a hospital in England to get **treatment**.

People around the world were **outraged** by this news and gave her a lot of support. Fortunately, she recovered from her **critical** condition. She was even **nominated** for the 2013 Nobel Peace Prize. On July 12, 2013, Malala's 16th birthday, she was invited to the UN to give a speech. She spoke in front of over 500 people from all around the world, and the UN announced that July 12 was Malala Day. Words 202

Q

What is the paragraph mainly about?

P1 What happened to a girl in ________

P2 Why Malala Yousafzai made the Taliban ________

P3 What happened to Malala Yousafzai after she (recovered / won a prize)

CHECK YOUR COMPREHENSION

Choose the best answers.

Main Idea

1 **What is the passage mainly about?**

a. The cruelty of the Taliban

b. Brave women around the world

c. A girl who fought for the right to be educated

d. The reality of education for women in Pakistan

Details

2 **Why did Malala write a blog for the BBC?**

a. Because she loved writing

b. Because the Taliban killed her family

c. Because she wanted to become famous

d. Because the Taliban did not allow girls to go to school

3 **Malala Day was announced on ________________.**

a. UN Day

b. Malala's birthday

c. the day Malala got shot

d. the day Malala recovered

4 **Which question CANNOT be answered from the passage?**

a. Where did Malala get shot?

b. How did Malala become famous?

c. What school was Malala attending?

d. What did Malala do on her 16th birthday?

Write the answers in complete sentences.

5 **Why was the Taliban upset with Malala?**

____

6 **What did the Taliban do to Malala?**

____

SHOW YOUR COMPREHENSION

Write the numbers in the correct order.

Malala Yousafzai

a. Malala was taken to a hospital in England. ______

b. The Taliban stopped girls from attending school. ______

c. The UN announced that July 12 was Malala Day. ______

d. Malala wrote a blog for the BBC about the Taliban's cruelty. ______

e. The Taliban shot her in the head and the neck on a school bus. ______

f. After her recovery, she was nominated for the Nobel Peace Prize. ______

g. She was invited to the UN to give a speech on her 16th birthday. ______

SUMMARIZE YOUR READING

Complete the summary with the words from the box.

Malala Day	recovery	attend school	shot
educated	cruelty	the UN	support

Malala Yousafzai is a Pakistani girl who fought for the right to be ❶ ______________. The Taliban did not allow girls to ❷ ______________. So she wrote a blog for the BBC to let the world know about the Taliban's ❸ ______________. This made the Taliban very upset, so they ❹ ______________ her in the head and the neck on a school bus. People around the world got very angry and gave her a lot of ❺ ______________. After her ❻ ______________, she was invited to ❼ ______________ to give a speech, and July 12, her birthday, was called ❽ ______________.

UNIT 20 | **Subject** Social Studies **Topic** Advertisements

I Will Catch Your Eye!

WARM UP
1. Why do people use advertisements?
2. How do advertisements affect our lives?

BEFORE YOU READ

A Match the words with the definitions below.

1. ______ catch one's eye a. to buy something
2. ______ bombard b. to get someone's attention
3. ______ promote c. to hit or attack again and again
4. ______ heroine d. to help sell a product or make it popular
5. ______ purchase e. a woman who is the main character in a book, film, etc.

B Background Knowledge

Many businesses advertise their stores as well as the goods and services they sell. They do this to increase sales and to let more people know about their companies. Print advertisements appear in newspapers and magazines. There are also TV and radio ads as well as online ads.

"Hey there! Look at me and buy me!"

Who is talking to you? Advertisements are. Companies make countless new products every day. To sell these new products, they try hard to **catch your eye**. Do you know how they do that?

What is the paragraph mainly about?

P2 Where we can see ______________

Every day, advertisers **bombard** you with ads. For instance, when you watch TV, commercial films talk to you. A number of posters are placed on buses and subways. When you surf the Internet, ads pop up. Simply put, advertisements are everywhere.

Others advertise their products in interesting ways. Even in the 19th century, advertisers did this. In 1897, a writer had just completed his first book. However, his publisher was not interested in **promoting** the book. One day, he went to a newspaper company. Then, he placed an ad. It read, "I am a young millionaire. I love sports and music. I am a very understanding person. And I want to marry a woman who resembles the **heroine** in W.S. Maugham's novel."

P3 How W.S. Maugham advertised (himself / his book)

The ad certainly caught the eyes of many women. In less than a week, every copy of W.S. Maugham's novel was **purchased**. What was the name of the advertiser? He was the novelist William Somerset Maugham. Words 199

P4 How (expensive / successful) W.S. Maugham's ad was

CHECK YOUR COMPREHENSION

Choose the best answers.

Main Idea

1 What is the passage mainly about?

a. How to advertise yourself
b. Ways to advertise new products
c. What makes a good advertisement
d. The influence of advertisements on our lives

Details

2 Which is NOT mentioned as a way to advertise a product?

a. By putting ads on TV
b. By putting ads in books
c. By putting ads in newspapers
d. By putting ads on public transportation

3 In paragraph 2, "advertisers bombard you with ads" is closest in meaning to ______________.

a. advertisements are harmful
b. advertisements are necessary
c. advertisements are in many places
d. advertisements attract our attention

4 Why did W.S. Maugham place an ad in the newspaper?

a. To get a job
b. To sell his novel
c. To marry a woman
d. To introduce himself

Write the answers in complete sentences.

5 Why did W.S. Maugham place an ad himself?

____

6 Was W.S. Maugham's ad successful? Why?

____

SHOW YOUR COMPREHENSION

Fill in the chart with the phrases from the box.

Advertising New Products

Putting Ads Everywhere	• ❶ ______________ on TV • posters placed on ❷ ______________ • ❸ ______________ on the Internet
Advertising in Interesting Ways	• e.g. W.S. Maugham's ad ❹ ______________

pop-up ads
buses and subways
commercial films
for his first book in a newspaper

SUMMARIZE YOUR READING

Complete the summary with the words from the box.

advertisements　　the Internet　　novel　　sold out
interesting　　eyes　　commercials　　heroine

Companies try to catch people's ❶ ______________ to sell their products. In some cases, they put ❷ ______________ everywhere people go. There are TV ❸ ______________, posters on buses and subways, and pop-up ads on ❹ ______________. In another case, people also advertise goods in ❺ ______________ ways. One example was the ad by a novelist W.S. Maugham. To sell his ❻ ______________, he placed an ad in the newspaper. It read, "I am a millionaire. I want to marry a woman like the ❼ ______________ in W.S. Maugham's novel." In less than a week, the book ❽ ______________.

THINK & WRITE 5

What Are Some Disadvantages of Advertisements?

STEP 1 **DISCUSSION** **Talk to your partner and answer the questions.**

1. Do you think advertisements are good or bad things?
2. What do advertisements do for us?

STEP 2 **ORGANIZATION** **Fill in the chart with the phrases from the box.**

wrong ideas about beauty	to buy more products
look like the unrealistic models	goods that we do not really need
advertisers sometimes tell lies	incorrect information about products

Introduction	Advertisements have several disadvantages.
Body	**Supporting sentence 1:** Advertisements encourage us ____________________. **Details:** As a result, we may buy ____________________. **Supporting sentence 2:** Advertisements may give us ____________________. **Details:** To sell their products, ____________________ that their products are perfect. **Supporting sentence 3:** Advertisements may give us ____________________. **Details:** Some people may try to ____________________ in advertisements.
Conclusion	Because of advertisements, we may buy unnecessary goods, get incorrect product information, and get wrong ideas about beauty.

STEP 3 FIRST DRAFT **Complete the writing with the phrases from the chart.**

Title What Are Some Disadvantages of Advertisements?

Advertisements have several disadvantages.

First, advertisements encourage us ______________________. As a result, we may buy ______________________.

Second, advertisements may give us ______________________. To sell their products, ______________________ that their products are perfect.

Lastly, advertisements may give us ______________________. Some people may try to ______________________ in advertisements.

Because of advertisements, we may buy unnecessary goods, get incorrect product information, and get wrong ideas about beauty.

STEP 4 FINAL DRAFT **Complete the writing. Replace one of the details with you own idea.**

Title ______________________

Advertisements have several disadvantages.

First, ______________________

____

Second, ______________________

____

Lastly, ______________________

____

Because of advertisements, we may ______________________

____

MEMO

MEMO

MEMO

MEMO

MEMO

School Subject-Integrated Reading Series

Reading for Subject

SECOND EDITION

Workbook

1

DARAKWON

School Subject-Integrated Reading Series

Reading for Subject

SECOND EDITION

Workbook

1

VOCABULARY PRACTICE

A Write the correct words for the definitions.

native	bark	layer	in pieces	cell

1. in separate parts ____________
2. the hard outer covering of a tree ____________
3. living or growing naturally in a place ____________
4. the smallest basic unit of a plant or animal ____________
5. a sheet of something that lies over another thing ____________

B Choose the word that has a meaning similar to the underlined word.

1. His performance during the game was really <u>amazing</u>.

   a. strange b. natural c. terrible d. surprising

2. We should not judge people by their <u>appearance</u>.

   a. looks b. clothes c. personality d. behavior

C Complete the sentences with the words in the box.

shed	trunk	thin	disappear	visible

1. Some stars are not ____________ with the naked eye.
2. Trees ____________ their leaves in autumn.
3. Watch out! The ice is too ____________ to walk on.
4. Branches are growing from the tree ____________.
5. The magician can make a rabbit ____________ in his hat.

SENTENCE PRACTICE

D **Translate the sentences into your language, focusing on the meanings of the underlined parts.**

1. One species, the rainbow eucalyptus, <u>is considered</u> the most beautiful tree in the world.

 ____

2. The pieces form different colors, <u>creating</u> the tree's rainbow-like appearance.

 ____

3. The cells in the layer have a pigment <u>called</u> tannin.

 ____

4. <u>As</u> the chlorophyll starts to disappear, the colors of the tannin become visible.

 ____

E **Unscramble the words to complete the sentences.**

1. is / Australia / the eucalyptus tree / native to

 ____

2. is / sheds / the rainbow eucalyptus / that / its bark / a tall tree

 ______________________________ every year.

3. amazing / happens / something

 After that, ______________________________

4. will / is / remember / a sight / people / always

 It ______________________________

VOCABULARY PRACTICE

A Write the correct words for the definitions.

bury	artisan	employ	suffer from	overlook

1. to hire; to pay a person to do work ______________
2. to experience something painful ______________
3. to place a dead body in the ground ______________
4. a skilled worker who makes things by hand ______________
5. to have a view of something, especially from above ______________

B Choose the word that has a meaning similar to the underlined word.

1. Everyone must obey the orders the <u>emperor</u> gave.

   a. ruler b. owner c. manager d. president

2. It is important to <u>complete</u> the work on time.

   a. help b. start c. review d. finish

C Complete the sentences with the words in the box.

gave birth to	promises	construction	poverty	overthrow

1. My aunt ______________ a healthy baby girl last night.
2. The ______________ of the building is taking a lot of time.
3. I do not like John because he never keeps his ______________.
4. Despite making progress, many people still live in ______________.
5. The rebels are trying to ______________ the government.

SENTENCE PRACTICE

D Translate the sentences into your language, focusing on the meanings of the underlined parts.

1. Before she died, she asked him to bury her in the most beautiful tomb in the world.

   ____

2. To keep his promise, Shah Jahan began to build the most beautiful tomb: the Taj Mahal.

   ____

3. In addition, he spent so much money that people suffered from poverty.

   ____

4. After that, Shah Jahan was kept in Fort Agra, which overlooked the Taj Mahal.

   ____

E Unscramble the words to complete the sentences.

1. loved / anyone else / he / more / her / than

   ____

2. giving birth to / Mumtaz Mahal / while / died / their child

   In 1631, however, ______________________________

3. Shah Jahan / the artisans' / craftsmen's / cut off / and / fingers

   Soon after the completion, ______________________________

4. afraid / build / would / that / in / they / the same tomb / another place

   He was ______________________________

VOCABULARY PRACTICE

A Write the correct words for the definitions.

effect	refer to	intelligence	improve	suggest

1. to make something better ______________
2. something produced by a cause ______________
3. the ability to learn and understand ______________
4. to propose doing something ______________
5. to mention or speak about something ______________

B Choose the word that has a meaning similar to the underlined word.

1. The teacher will <u>describe</u> the problem for the students.

   a. solve b. correct c. explain d. announce

2. Let's try to <u>reduce</u> the amount of pollution we create.

   a. limit b. lower c. check d. throw away

C Complete the sentences with the words in the box.

worked	mistakenly	mental	governor	relaxed

1. Sleep is important for ______________ and physical health.
2. The man is the ______________ of California, USA.
3. Lying in the sun makes me feel happy and ______________.
4. I ______________ called her Hani instead of Hana.
5. The medicine ______________ and made John feel better.

SENTENCE PRACTICE

D **Translate the sentences into your language, focusing on the meanings of the underlined parts.**

1. The Mozart Effect refers to the belief <u>that</u> listening to Mozart's music can make people smarter.

   ____

2. Then, in 1993, the researchers Shaw and Ky studied <u>whether</u> the Mozart Effect really worked.

   ____

3. Don Campbell also said that stress and depression <u>could be reduced</u> and that people <u>could be relaxed</u> by listening to Mozart's music.

   ____

4. But <u>it</u> is certain <u>that</u> listening to Mozart's music <u>helps you be</u> calm and <u>focus</u> on your studies.

   ____

E **Unscramble the words to complete the sentences.**

1. very / was once / mothers / it / with / popular

   ____

2. played / possible / their babies / they / Mozart's music / to / as much as

   ____

3. Alfred A. Tomatis / was / by / the Mozart Effect / first described

   ______________________________ in 1991.

4. the Mozart Effect / has / of / the popularity / disappeared

   ______________________________ today.

VOCABULARY PRACTICE

A Write the correct words for the definitions.

order	patty	spread	cattle	stomach

1. to ask for food or drink in a restaurant ______________
2. cows kept on a farm for their meat or milk ______________
3. the organ in the body where food is digested ______________
4. a small, flat piece of cooked meat or other food ______________
5. to scatter; to distribute over an area ______________

B Choose the word that has a meaning similar to the underlined word.

1. The hunters are trying to <u>trap</u> the lion in the village.

   a. find b. watch c. scare d. capture

2. The world leaders will discuss how to <u>combat</u> climate change.

   a. study b. fight c. monitor d. change

C Complete the sentences with the words in the box.

heat	breathe	fill up with	burp	instead of

1. I was unable to ______________ because of the smoke.
2. The sun provides us with light and ______________.
3. We decided to take a taxi ______________ a bus.
4. It is rude to ______________ at the table in some countries.
5. It takes time for the pool to ______________ water.

SENTENCE PRACTICE

D **Translate the sentences into your language, focusing on the meanings of the underlined parts.**

1. Your order can make the Earth even hotter.

2. To do that, John Martin, a scientist at the Moss Landing Marine Lab, suggested spreading iron into the sea.

3. As they need CO_2 to breathe, there would be fewer greenhouse gases.

4. In Estonia, there is a fart tax law to reduce the amount of methane produced by cattle.

E **Unscramble the words to complete the sentences.**

1. have / of / you / heard / greenhouse gases

   Maybe ______

2. to / people around / them / trying / the world / combat / are

   So ______

3. and / the most / of them / methane / famous / are

   Carbon dioxide ______

4. from / and burping / cannot really / we / cattle / farting / stop

   However, ______

I VOCABULARY PRACTICE

A Write the correct words for the definitions.

originate	create	source	for instance	violet

1. a color made by mixing blue and purple ________________
2. to make something new ________________
3. as an example ________________
4. a person, place, or thing that something comes from ________________
5. to start or arise ________________

B Choose the word that has a meaning similar to the underlined word.

1. The work of art has a number of different <u>hues</u> in it.

   a. lines b. colors c. shapes d. paintings

2. The chef <u>combines</u> the ingredients to make the cake.

   a. cuts b. cooks c. mixes d. chooses

C Complete the sentences with the words in the box.

interestingly	primary	paint	magenta	own

1. I wish I had my ________________ room.
2. Red, yellow, and blue are the ________________ colors.
3. ________________, there are penguins that live in Africa.
4. The artist mixed red and purple to get ________________.
5. He squeezed some ________________ onto the palette.

SENTENCE PRACTICE

D **Translate the sentences into your language, focusing on the meanings of the underlined parts.**

1. The room you are inside may have colors <u>such as</u> red, blue, green, yellow, and brown.

   ____

2. Most colors are created <u>by mixing</u> two or more together.

   ____

3. While these three <u>cannot be made</u> from other colors, they are actually the source of all other colors.

   ____

4. The three colors <u>formed</u> by mixing two primary colors are called secondary colors.

   ____

E **Unscramble the words to complete the sentences.**

1. all originate / these hues / from / three colors

   Interestingly, ______________________________

2. be / that way / cannot / three colors / created

   However, ______________________________

3. take / mix / some red / the two / and yellow paint / together / and

   ____

4. mix / you / get / yellow and blue / you / green

   If ______________________________

VOCABULARY PRACTICE

A Write the correct words for the definitions.

term	dig up	scholar	mystery	ancient

1. very old ______________
2. something that is not understood ______________
3. to take something out of the ground ______________
4. a word or expression with a particular meaning ______________
5. a person who knows a lot about a certain subject ______________

B Choose the word that has a meaning similar to the underlined word.

1. The archaeologist is trying to <u>decipher</u> the message on the tomb.

   a. write b. leave c. change d. translate

2. The stars on the American flag <u>stand for</u> the 50 states.

   a. hold b. mean c. point to d. look like

C Complete the sentences with the words in the box.

key	solve	army	symbol	civilization

1. Studying hard is the ______________ to his success.
2. A four-leaf clover is a(n) ______________ of good luck.
3. What should we do to ______________ the problem?
4. An ancient ______________ developed by the Nile River.
5. He served in the U.S. ______________ during World War II.

SENTENCE PRACTICE

D **Translate the sentences into your language, focusing on the meanings of the underlined parts.**

1. You may not feel good if someone compares you to a stone.

2. In 1822, the mystery finally began to be solved by French scholar Jean Francois Champollion.

3. However, thinking differently, Champollion found out that a single picture symbol could stand for a sound as well as a word.

4. Without it, we would not understand much about the ancient Egyptian language and civilization.

E **Unscramble the words to complete the sentences.**

1. solving / often / a key / this term / to / refers to / a problem

2. in / the same message / there / written / was / three different scripts

   On the stone, ________

3. easy / was / to / the hieroglyphics / not / understand

   However, it ________

4. that / was / most scholars / hieroglyphics / believed / picture writing

   At that time, ________

VOCABULARY PRACTICE

A Write the correct words for the definitions.

thorn	horn	nectar	invader	attract

1. a sharp point that grows on the stem of a plant ______________
2. a sweet liquid produced by flowers ______________
3. a curved, pointed growth on the head of an animal ______________
4. to make someone or something go somewhere ______________
5. a person or group that enters a place by force ______________

B Choose the word that has a meaning similar to the underlined word.

1. The tree trunk was <u>hollowed out</u> by a squirrel to make a nest.

   a. dug out   b. cut down   c. taken over   d. moved around

2. It is rude to <u>disturb</u> people studying in the library.

   a. greet   b. bother   c. look at   d. listen to

C Complete the sentences with the words in the box.

scold	protect	insects	attack	chemicals

1. The lions are going to ______________ the herd of zebras.
2. Teachers sometimes ______________ students who talk too much in class.
3. All ______________ have three body parts and six legs.
4. Cigarette smoke contains dangerous ______________.
5. You need to wear sunscreen to ______________ your skin from the sun.

SENTENCE PRACTICE

D **Translate the sentences into your language, focusing on the meanings of the underlined parts.**

1. Owen has an older sister <u>named</u> Cathy.

2. A similar type of behavior happens with bullhorn acacia trees and the ants <u>living</u> within them.

3. So the tree's flowers produce sweet nectar <u>to attract</u> bees.

4. But <u>what if</u> the ants still move onto the flowers?

E **Unscramble the words to complete the sentences.**

1. pretends / often / to / he / her / be / bodyguard

   So

2. look / they / a bull's / like / horns

3. must be / in order to / the tree / pollinated / make seeds

4. chemicals / to / produces / that are / it / ants / repellent

I VOCABULARY PRACTICE

A Write the correct words for the definitions.

prison	miss	weak	bucket	tradition

1. an open container with a handle ______________
2. not physically strong ______________
3. to feel sad that a person is not present ______________
4. a place where people who break the law must stay ______________
5. a way of acting that people have done for a long time ______________

B Choose the word that has a meaning similar to the underlined word.

1. I need some time to think about your <u>proposal</u>.

   a. job　　b. praise　　c. interest　　d. suggestion

2. We hope the couple live happily <u>ever after</u>.

   a. soon　　b. finally　　c. forever　　d. later

C Complete the sentences with the words in the box.

underground	spilled	serve	face	bride

1. The ______________ is wearing a white wedding dress.
2. The sofa can ______________ as a bed for guests.
3. The waiter ______________ water on my pants by mistake.
4. All rooms in this hotel ______________ the ocean.
5. The building has six floors and a(n) ______________ parking garage.

SENTENCE PRACTICE

D **Translate the sentences into your language, focusing on the meanings of the underlined parts.**

1. Her father became angry and put the goldsmith into an underground prison.

2. As the girl missed him, she became weak.

3. Tell him to make a cup two people can drink from at the same time.

4. As a result, two people could drink without spilling anything, and the couple finally got married.

E **Unscramble the words to complete the sentences.**

1. spilled / should / single drop / be / a

   Not

2. people / impossible / was / thought / this task

3. the goldsmith / true love / it / his / of / did

   But because

4. and it / held / raised arms / as / a bucket / a second cup / served

   Her

VOCABULARY PRACTICE

A Write the correct words for the definitions.

disaster	tragic	rescue	ash	ruins

1. very sad ______________
2. the gray powder left after something burns ______________
3. to save someone from a dangerous situation ______________
4. an event that results in great harm, damage, or death ______________
5. the broken parts that are left of an ancient building or town ______________

B Choose the word that has a meaning similar to the underlined word.

1. It was one of the most <u>destructive</u> earthquakes in history.

   a. recent b. famous c. harmful d. uncommon

2. The <u>eruption</u> of Mount St. Helens caused a great amount of damage.

   a. height b. location c. discovery d. explosion

C Complete the sentences with the words in the box.

destroyed	politicians	excavation	moisture	tourist attractions

1. The hurricane ______________ hundreds of houses.
2. There is a lot of ______________ in the air after it rains.
3. The Eiffel Tower is one of the top ______________ in Paris.
4. ______________ should serve the people of the country.
5. The ______________ of the buried city lasted several years.

SENTENCE PRACTICE

D **Translate the sentences into your language, focusing on the meanings of the underlined parts.**

1. Volcanoes, hurricanes, and earthquakes are called natural disasters because they cause people to die or to lose everything.

   ____

2. It is true that nature is more powerful than humans.

   ____

3. So by looking at them, people can see how people in ancient Rome lived.

   ____

4. Today, Pompeii is one of the most popular tourist attractions in Italy.

   ____

E **Unscramble the words to complete the sentences.**

1. natural disasters / destructive / can / how / shows / be

   The following story ______________________________

2. destroyed / of / Mount Vesuvius / because / the eruption / was / of

   In 79 A.D., Pompeii ______________________________

3. had / for / the ruins of Pompeii / well preserved / hundreds of / been / years

   ____

4. visit / every year / people / the city / 2.5 million

   About ______________________________

VOCABULARY PRACTICE

A Write the correct words for the definitions.

knowledge	guess	artist	opinion	worry

1. a person who creates art ____________
2. to give an answer which may not be true ____________
3. a person's belief or thought about something ____________
4. the information or facts that a person knows ____________
5. to keep thinking about problems or unpleasant things ____________

B Choose the word that has a meaning similar to the underlined word.

1. The students asked the teacher for some study <u>tips</u> for the test.

   a. gifts b. advice c. books d. products

2. Mr. Jackson is a world-famous <u>expert</u> on ancient Egypt.

   a. teacher b. reporter c. historian d. specialist

C Complete the sentences with the words in the box.

on display	share	rent	statue	pose

1. Michelangelo's most famous ____________ is *David*.
2. They will ____________ for a picture in front of the building.
3. The museum has many old cars ____________.
4. Jack and I ____________ a common interest in books.
5. You can ____________ a bicycle to ride around town.

SENTENCE PRACTICE

D **Translate the sentences into your language, focusing on the meanings of the underlined parts.**

1. First, you <u>do not have to be</u> an expert to enjoy art.

____

2. Second, renting an audio guide is another way <u>to enjoy</u> art museums.

____

3. Knowing a lot about art <u>makes people have</u> more fun in art museums.

____

4. So do not worry but just <u>allow yourself to enjoy</u> the art.

____

E **Unscramble the words to complete the sentences.**

1. are / enjoying / here / several tips / for / art museums

____

2. on display / try / see / not / every piece / to / art / of

Do _______________

3. were / the artists / in / trying / what / to say / their pictures

It may be fun to guess _______________

4. much better / will / you / the art / understand / make

It _______________

VOCABULARY PRACTICE

A Write the correct words for the definitions.

whisper	actor	perform	negative	bow

1. bad or harmful ______________
2. to speak quietly ______________
3. someone whose job is to act in plays or films ______________
4. to do something in front of an audience to entertain them ______________
5. to bend the head or upper body forward to greet or show respect to someone ______________

B Choose the word that has a meaning similar to the underlined word.

1. Mary always gets <u>nervous</u> before an exam.

   a. tired b. angry c. excited d. worried

2. I thought the movie was <u>excellent</u> and really enjoyed it.

   a. great b. strange c. terrible d. interesting

C Complete the sentences with the words in the box.

presentation	superstitious	dates back to	knee	cheered

1. I gave a ______________ in history class.
2. Jason hurt his ______________ while he was playing football.
3. Some ______________ people are afraid of black cats.
4. The origin of the festival ______________ the 12th century.
5. Everyone in the audience ______________ when the play ended.

SENTENCE PRACTICE

D **Translate the sentences into your language, focusing on the meanings of the underlined parts.**

1. You feel very nervous <u>as</u> you walk onto the stage.

2. Why does she <u>want me to break</u> my leg?

3. <u>The reason was that</u> stage actors were very superstitious.

4. <u>The better</u> the performance was, <u>the more</u> often the actors broke their legs.

E **Unscramble the words to complete the sentences.**

1. is / your classmates / it / to make / your turn / a presentation / in front of

2. back / explanation / dates / time / another / William Shakespeare's / to

3. by bending / "break a leg" / the phrase / bowing / meant / at the knee

   In those days, ____________________

4. the phrase / said / success / wish / in / was / to / them / their performances

   Therefore, ____________________

VOCABULARY PRACTICE

A Write the correct words for the definitions.

be about to	reality	owner	flight	cost

1. a person who owns something ______________
2. to have the price of ______________
3. the state of being real ______________
4. a trip on a plane, helicopter, spaceship, etc. ______________
5. to be ready to do something ______________

B Choose the word that has a meaning similar to the underlined word.

1. The passengers on board were mostly Asians.

   a. mainly b. closely c. probably d. especially

2. The trip was canceled due to a problem with the car.

   a. after b. next to c. because of d. instead of

C Complete the sentences with the words in the box.

tourists	founder	surface	ambitious	go down

1. He is ______________ and wants to be a CEO.
2. She is the ______________ of a clothing company.
3. The elevator will _______ _______ to the first floor.
4. Leaves are floating on the ______________ of the lake.
5. The ______________ enjoyed their time at the museum.

SENTENCE PRACTICE

D Translate the sentences into your language, focusing on the meanings of the underlined parts.

1. Millions of people have dreamed of traveling into space since they first looked up at the night sky.

2. This is about to become reality for some of them.

3. The least expensive one costs $200,000.

4. Soon, going into space may be almost as cheap as flying across an ocean.

E Unscramble the words to complete the sentences.

1. outer space / became / Yuri Gagarin / the first man / in

   In 1961, ______

2. mostly / this / due to / is / three men

3. showed / were / their companies / that / take / ready to / tourists / into space

   But they ______

4. that is / above / eighty kilometers / than / the Earth's surface / more

VOCABULARY PRACTICE

A Write the correct words for the definitions.

plenty of	regret	assistant	failure	prepare

1. a lack of success ________
2. to make plans for a future event ________
3. enough or more than enough ________
4. to feel sorry about something you did ________
5. a person whose job is to help with someone's work ________

B Choose the word that has a meaning similar to the underlined word.

1. William Shakespeare coined many words in his plays.

   a. wrote   b. missed   c. created   d. changed

2. They have different views on how to raise their children.

   a. tips   b. skills   c. opinions   d. experiences

C Complete the sentences with the words in the box.

went wrong	screamed	named after	carried out	injury

1. She ________ when she saw a bug in her food.
2. My plan to give her a surprise party ________.
3. The Nobel Prizes were ________ Alfred Nobel.
4. He suffered a(n) ________ during the soccer game.
5. They ________ a survey of 100 high school students.

SENTENCE PRACTICE

D **Translate the sentences into your language, focusing on the meanings of the underlined parts.**

1. Murphy's Law is not something <u>that</u> law school students need to know.

2. The expression <u>is</u> often <u>used to mean</u> "If anything can go wrong, it will."

3. Then, you <u>regret changing</u> lines.

4. <u>Not happy with the failure</u>, Murphy said about the assistant, "If there is any way to make a mistake, he will."

E **Unscramble the words to complete the sentences.**

1. who / is not / the expression / clear / it / first coined

2. was / important test / carrying out / he / an

   One day, ______________________

3. assistant / because / a mistake / failed / made / one

   It ______________________

4. thought / Murphy's Law / can / things / about / that / go wrong

   We always ______________________

VOCABULARY PRACTICE

A Write the correct words for the definitions.

predict	damage	burrow	observe	toad

1. an animal like a frog that has dry, rough skin ________
2. to make a guess about a future event ________
3. to see or look at, often carefully ________
4. a hole or tunnel that an animal digs to live in ________
5. injury or harm ________

B Choose the word that has a meaning similar to the underlined word.

1. The game will <u>take place</u> at 7:00 this evening.

   a. host b. show c. end d. happen

2. Martin will <u>depart</u> his home in London on Friday morning.

   a. sell b. leave c. build d. decorate

C Complete the sentences with the words in the box.

scared	strikes	hibernate	detect	exceptional

1. Lightning sometimes ________ when it is not raining.
2. The girl has a(n) ________ talent for languages.
3. The horses were ________ because of the loud noise.
4. The cameras can ________ anyone in the building.
5. Bears and squirrels often ________ in winter.

SENTENCE PRACTICE

D **Translate the sentences into your language, focusing on the meanings of the underlined parts.**

1. Scientists have observed other animals acting strangely before natural disasters.

   ____

2. One is that animals can sense tremors in the ground.

   ____

3. And some animals, such as dogs, have exceptional hearing.

   ____

4. This lets them know about natural disasters, too.

   ____

E **Unscramble the words to complete the sentences.**

1. occurred / other / have / in / events / places

   Similar ______________________________

2. in / can / air pressure / other animals / changes / detect

   ____

3. tells / is / or typhoon / a hurricane / coming / them

   That ______________________________

4. acting / your dog / strangely / be / no reason / starts / careful / for

   So if ______________________________

VOCABULARY PRACTICE

A Write the correct words for the definitions.

differ	ceremony	strict	personality	recognize

1. not to be the same as ____________
2. a person's characteristics ____________
3. not able to be changed or broken ____________
4. to know or remember someone or something ____________
5. a formal activity conducted for a special event ____________

B Choose the word that has a meaning similar to the underlined word.

1. People say that red roses <u>represent</u> love and passion.

   a. mean b. cover c. look like d. celebrate

2. Some people believe there are evil <u>spirits</u> in the ruins of the city.

   a. rulers b. ghosts c. people d. monsters

C Complete the sentences with the words in the box.

disguise	class	character	return	communicate

1. The rich man belongs to the upper ____________.
2. He is going to ____________ to his own country next year.
3. The thief's ____________ kept everyone from recognizing him.
4. In the past, people often used letters to ____________.
5. The main ____________ in the movie is very brave and smart.

SENTENCE PRACTICE

D **Translate the sentences into your language, focusing on the meanings of the underlined parts.**

1. You may have watched a program on TV in which African people wearing masks were dancing in a ceremony.

   ____

2. Masks differ from country to country and have been used for various reasons.

   ____

3. Therefore, wearing masks gave people the chance to hide which class they were in.

   ____

4. The Egyptians believed each mask could help a soul recognize its body and return to it.

   ____

E **Unscramble the words to complete the sentences.**

1. in / used / people / masks / traditional dances

   In Korea, ______________________________

2. take / in / would / great joy / mocking / through / the ruling class / mask dances

   They ______________________________

3. were / dead people's / put / they / faces / on

   ____

4. it / masks / seems / one thing / have / that / in common

   ____

VOCABULARY PRACTICE

A Write the correct words for the definitions.

dessert	fortune	contain	lottery	saying

1. to have or hold inside ______________
2. sweet food eaten at the end of a meal ______________
3. the good or bad things that happen in life ______________
4. a proverb or something similar people say ______________
5. a game in which people buy numbered tickets ______________

B Choose the word that has a meaning similar to the underlined word.

1. The strong man can <u>split</u> a log into two with his axe.

   a. lift b. push c. drag d. divide

2. Let's go to the same museum we visited on our <u>previous</u> trip here.

   a. first b. prior c. exciting d. important

C Complete the sentences with the words in the box.

message	inside	temple	immigrants	introduced

1. His car was locked, and the keys were ______________.
2. She was in a meeting, so I left a(n) ______________.
3. I like to visit the ______________ because I feel calm there.
4. Cotton was first ______________ to Korea in the 14th century.
5. They are ______________ to Canada and come from Spain.

SENTENCE PRACTICE

D **Translate the sentences into your language, focusing on the meanings of the underlined parts.**

1. We call this cookie a fortune cookie.

 ____

2. People enjoy them because it is fun to read the messages on the paper.

 ____

3. Although you may think that they are from China, there are no fortune cookies in China.

 ____

4. They are based on *omikuji*, which was used in Japanese temples in the 19th century.

 ____

E **Unscramble the words to complete the sentences.**

1. tells / the message / you / on the paper / your fortune

 ____

2. winning lottery numbers / the lists of / contain / previous / lucky numbers

 In addition, ______________________________

3. for dessert / often serve / in the United States / fortune cookies / Chinese restaurants

 ____

4. they / Chinese restaurants / by / popularized / there / were

 Then, ______________________________

VOCABULARY PRACTICE

A Write the correct words for the definitions.

mess up	truth	hide	gesture	confident

1. a statement of fact ______________
2. to make something untidy or dirty ______________
3. to prevent something from being seen ______________
4. feeling sure of oneself or one's abilities ______________
5. a body movement that has a certain meaning ______________

B Choose the word that has a meaning similar to the underlined word.

1. John is certainly the most talented player on the team.

   a. never b. possibly c. definitely d. carefully

2. The students feel a bit anxious about their test.

   a. calm b. nervous c. upset d. pleased

C Complete the sentences with the words in the box.

lies	prove	means	unwilling	steeple

1. Honest people do not tell ______________ to others.
2. The church has a very pointy ______________.
3. You must ______________ that you are telling the truth.
4. John was ______________ to talk about the problem.
5. Email is a modern ______________ of communication people use.

SENTENCE PRACTICE

D **Translate the sentences into your language, focusing on the meanings of the underlined parts.**

1. They proved <u>that</u> your nose gets warm when you tell a lie.

2. <u>As for</u> the other parts of your body, your hands say a lot.

3. For example, <u>covering</u> your mouth with a hand may mean you are hiding something.

4. So you cover your mouth to <u>stop yourself from telling</u> more lies.

E **Unscramble the words to complete the sentences.**

1. Pinocchio's / is / growing / your nose / not / like

   Certainly, __________

2. we / our bodies / ourselves / to / understood / also use / make

3. putting / you are / your hands / something / unwilling / may mean / in your pockets / to do

4. you / shows / hand gesture / that / confident / this / are

VOCABULARY PRACTICE

A Write the correct words for the definitions.

virus	global	limited	community	affect

1. happening in all parts of the world __________
2. to have an influence on someone or something __________
3. a tiny organism that often causes diseases __________
4. small in amount or number __________
5. all the people living in a particular area __________

B Choose the word that has a meaning similar to the underlined word.

1. It is <u>nearly</u> time for the game to start.

   a. exactly　b. almost　c. roughly　d. perfectly

2. Sue traveled around the <u>entire</u> country during her vacation.

   a. whole　b. nearby　c. foreign　d. interesting

C Complete the sentences with the words in the box.

disease	rapidly	infect	outbreak	multiple

1. There is a flu __________ at the local school.
2. The doctors hope to cure the __________ soon.
3. Some viruses can __________ people easily.
4. It is boring to watch a movie __________ times.
5. His business has grown __________ in the last two years.

SENTENCE PRACTICE

D **Translate the sentences into your language, focusing on the meanings of the underlined parts.**

1. An epidemic is an outbreak of a disease <u>that</u> spreads quickly in a limited area.

2. Other pandemics <u>made many people sick</u> but killed smaller numbers of them.

3. <u>Not all</u> epidemics become pandemics.

4. But pandemics <u>do spread</u> widely and infect many people.

E **Unscramble the words to complete the sentences.**

1. but / many people / do not / large numbers / them / kill / of

   Others infect ______________________________

2. may / a pandemic / or even / multiple countries / affect / the entire world

   ____

3. Europe's population / up to / was / half of / dead

   When it ended, ______________________________

4. always / neither / millions of / kills / people

   And ______________________________

VOCABULARY PRACTICE

A Write the correct words for the definitions.

shoot	shock	recover	support	announce

1. to fire a gun ______________
2. to officially tell people something ______________
3. to get well again after being ill or hurt ______________
4. to make someone feel upset or surprised ______________
5. the act of helping someone by giving love, encouragement, etc. ______________

B Choose the word that has a meaning similar to the underlined word.

1. Jane hopes to <u>attend</u> a good university next year.

   a. visit b. go to c. leave d. find out

2. Kevin is in <u>critical</u> condition after the car accident.

   a. calm b. serious c. perfect d. nervous

C Complete the sentences with the words in the box.

worldwide	treatment	outraged	speech	nominated

1. After the ______________, his pain has gone away.
2. People were all ______________ by the terrorist attack.
3. She will give a(n) ______________ about how to help the poor.
4. The movie made him famous ______________.
5. He was ______________ for the best actor award this year.

SENTENCE PRACTICE

D **Translate the sentences into your language, focusing on the meanings of the underlined parts.**

1. This news shocked people around the world, and they wanted to know more about <u>who she was</u> and <u>why she got shot</u>.

   ____

2. In the Swat Valley, the Taliban <u>had stopped girls from attending</u> school.

   ____

3. She nearly died, and she was moved to a hospital in England <u>to get</u> treatment.

   ____

4. People around the world were outraged by this news and <u>gave her a lot of support</u>.

   ____

E **Unscramble the words to complete the sentences.**

1. her / returning / while / was / she / home / shot / on a school bus

   They ______________________________

2. from / she / critical / recovered / her / condition

   Fortunately, ______________________________

3. was / for / even nominated / she / the 2013 Nobel Peace Prize.

   ____

4. to / a speech / invited / she / the UN / was / give / to

   On July 12, 2013, Malala's 16th birthday, ______________________________

VOCABULARY PRACTICE

A Write the correct words for the definitions.

countless	commercial	publisher	novel	understanding

1. too many in number ______________
2. kind and forgiving ______________
3. a company that prints books or magazines ______________
4. relating to the buying and selling of goods ______________
5. a story about imaginary characters and events ______________

B Choose the word that has a meaning similar to the underlined word.

1. There are <u>a number of</u> problems with my computer.

   a. a few   b. many   c. small   d. several

2. She <u>resembles</u> her mother very closely.

   a. helps   b. dislikes   c. looks like   d. lives with

C Complete the sentences with the words in the box.

advertise	millionaire	marry	heroin	purchased

1. He ______________ the car for half price.
2. The man asked the woman to ______________ him.
3. Many companies ______________ their products online these days.
4. The ______________ of the story is a young girl named Dorothy.
5. John became a(n) ______________ because his business was successful.

SENTENCE PRACTICE

D **Translate the sentences into your language, focusing on the meanings of the underlined parts.**

1. <u>To sell</u> these new products, they try hard to catch your eye.

   ____

2. A number of posters <u>are placed</u> on buses and subways.

   ____

3. <u>Simply put</u>, advertisements are everywhere.

   ____

4. I want to marry a woman <u>who</u> resembles the heroine in W.S. Maugham's novel.

   ____

E **Unscramble the words to complete the sentences.**

1. bombard / with / advertisers / you / ads

   Every day, ______________________________

2. had / a writer / just / first book / completed / his

   In 1897, ______________________________

3. was / in / the book / interested / promoting / his publisher / not

   However, ______________________________

4. the eyes / certainly / many / the ad / women / caught / of

   ____

MEMO

MEMO

MEMO

Reading for Subject

SECOND EDITION